Round Table

Round Table

by JOHN McEVOY

THOROUGHBRED
Legends®
No. 16

ECLIPSE
PRESS

Lexington, Kentucky

Library of Congress Control Number: 2001096889

ISBN 1-58150-072-6

Printed in The United States
First Edition: May 2002

Distributed to the trade by
National Book Network
4720-A Boston Way
Lanham, MD 20706
1.800.462.6420

a division of
The Blood-Horse, Inc.
PUBLISHERS SINCE 1916

To learn more about Round Table
and other classic Thoroughbreds, see:

www.thoroughbredlegends.com

ROUND TABLE

CONTENTS

INTRODUCTION

"A Little Machine"

M y formative days as a racing fan and horse player were brightened by the influential presence of
a bar owner and bookmaker named Angelo Salerno,
whose combined place of business was in my home-
town of Kenosha, Wisconsin.

Angelo, son of hard-working Sicilian immigrants,
decided after his much-decorated service as a sergeant
in the U.S. Marines during World War II that the long
tradition of tough physical labor maintained by the
men in his family was going to come to a halt — with
him. At one time an avid horseplayer but terrible bet-
tor, he decided to "go to the other side of the counter,"
as he put it, "and take advantage of suckers like you
guys." So he started booking horse bets, eventually
accumulating the wherewithal to purchase a modest-
sized saloon for use as headquarters. The only police-

man I ever saw in the place would come in to eat a free lunch and bet the Southern California tracks.

Kenosha was a blue-collar town, home in those days to such manufacturing companies as American Motors, American Brass Co., Simmons Mattress, and Angelo was a blue-collar bookie with a simple business motto: "Pay up or die."

I doubt that Angelo meant this literally, but there was no question that with his big hands, jutting jaw, and blazing black eyes he inspired respect. One day Angelo accepted what was for him a large bet — $150 — from the barber across the street. The bet was on a solid favorite. Angelo was unable to reach his layoff man in Milwaukee, and he didn't want to get stuck with the wager, so he gave the money to a regular customer named Frank Andreoli, who was going to Arlington Park that afternoon, instructing him to "put it on the six horse in the fifth race." The horse ran out.

Weeks later, Frank confided to me that he had made a mistake at Arlington that day: he bet the $150 on the *five* horse in the *sixth* race. This serendipitous error resulted in Frank's collecting $425, which he happily pocketed. Frank emphasized that Angelo must never be told of this. I naively inquired if Frank had considered giving Angelo "at least a part" of his accidental winnings. Frank responded with an incredulous look and then a loud laugh, before adding: "If that horse he wanted me to bet had won, and I couldn't pay after I screwed up, what parts of me do you think Angelo would have settled for?"

Angelo's only brush with the law came when he was cited for not having a federal gambling stamp and was ordered to appear in court in Milwaukee. Angelo hauled out his old Marine uniform and took it to Puntillo the tailor, who labored long and hard to let out enough material to accommodate its now bulkier owner. When Angelo strode into the courtroom and saluted the judge, who turned out to be another ex-Marine, the case against him was summarily dismissed.

Over the years Angelo developed a discernible disdain for much of his clientele. And his interest in racing was pretty much confined to encouraging his customers to "go on and keep betting those bums." His outlook on horses was decidedly unsentimental. They were just numbers to him, numbers that he could usually rely on his customers to misinterpret.

The only horses Angelo revealed any affection for were those who always appeared to be "sitting on a win," but stayed sitting; and he hated those few that consistently performed well. As a result, there developed at the Chicago tracks in the late 1950s a target of what could be Angelo's considerable ire — a horse on whom Angelo's customers almost always won. This horse became Angelo's nemesis, then near-obsession (and an obsessed Sicilian bookmaker is not a comforting presence). The object of Angelo's hatred was Round Table.

From ages three through five, Round Table made nineteen starts at Chicago tracks, winning fifteen, finishing second twice and third once, with four of the victories coming in betless exhibitions. (Round Table had gone one for three there as a two-year-old.)

Most of my friends and I were relatively new to horse racing when Round Table emerged as a star. So, he was our first "good horse," one whose races we eagerly awaited, one that we talked about frequently — in other words, our first equine hero.

My gang of horseplayers got onto the Round Table-in-Chicago factor early and bet him accordingly. Even when we were going to drive down to either Arlington or Washington parks to watch Round Table in action, we would leave bets with Angelo just to irritate him.

"Why does he have to run every week?" Angelo once lamented, for it seemed like every week to him.

Arlington Park was our favorite destination because of its proximity and ambience. When you looked out from Arlington's vast wooden grandstand in those days, the view across the racing strip to the south and west was of corn and hay fields. Arlington's paddock then was dotted with tall trees, as Keeneland's is today, and the horses were saddled beneath a canopy of leaves.

One of the regulars in Angelo's bar was a ne'er-do-well Ivy League graduate named Tupper Bailey, who lived on a generous trust fund and an equally formidable reliance on martinis. He made ten one-hundred-dollar show bets on Round Table in the 1957 to 1959 Chicago races and won them all.

This drove Angelo nuts. It wasn't that he was forced to pay out a great deal of money to Tupper; rather, it was the principle of the thing — bettors aren't supposed to beat their bookies like a drum.

The only time Round Table failed to finish in the money at the Chicago tracks from 1957 to 1959 — in the Equipoise Handicap of 1958, when he was fifth, beaten four lengths under 131 pounds — Tupper was undergoing one of his periodic drying out periods at a Milwaukee hospital. Upon his return, Angelo greeted him with "I put you down for your usual bet on Round Table; you lost." Tupper dismissed this attempt by Angelo with a curt, "You're out of your mind."

A turning point in our relationship with Salerno came in the summer of 1959. As a grizzled Marine veteran, saloon keeper, his own bouncer, and a cynical businessman, Angelo probably found us interesting only as curiosities. We were all young college students then, some of us working our summers on road construction, others at typewriters, all of us playing softball (Salerno sponsored our team) and horses, and all hanging out with Angelo — because we spent so much time in his place. He didn't hang out with us — he had to be there. But I'm pretty sure he liked us. We paid our bar tabs and bet tabs on time, and while we respected him we also razzed the hell out of him — especially when he had to pay off a wager to one of us.

On June 13, 1959, Angelo finally accepted one of our repeated invitations to join us on a trip south to see Round Table run. It was the Citation Handicap at old Washington Park, eighty miles from Kenosha. I will never forget that afternoon, for what happened indelibly impressed upon me the power of a horse — observed in person — to transform indifference into respect and passion in even the most hardened observer.

Angelo paid hardly any attention to the early races on the card, and he spent the sixth and seventh flirting with the lady bartender at the beer stand near where we sat.

He rejoined us as the field paraded for the Citation. Eyes narrowed, he gave Round Table a long look. "So that's your so-called Big Horse, eh?" he scoffed. "Not a whole lot to him is there?"

The tune changed as the race unfolded. Under Steve Brooks, Round Table won a stretch duel with Etonian to score by a neck at 4-5. Round Table, giving the runner-up a whopping twenty-six pounds and exhibiting the grit and determination that were hallmarks of his career, would not be denied. The crowd cheered the finish and applauded Round Table as he returned.

The effect of this on Angelo was dramatic. Face flushed, he watched intently as Round Table came back to be unsaddled. "He's a tough little son of a bitch, I'll give you that," he told us. Shaking his head, Angelo added: "He's like a little machine; he just keeps coming."

During the ride home that evening, Angelo commented repeatedly, almost to himself as he looked out the car window, on what he had witnessed at Washington Park. He had questions about Round Table's record, which we gladly answered, sensing a convert — and an unlikely one at that — in our midst.

As we pulled into the parking lot behind his Kenosha tavern, Angelo astounded us when he announced, "Boys, the drinks are on me. Thanks for showing me that little horse. He works hard, just like my old man did...like a little machine."

From that day on, there was no more staunch admirer of Round Table than the bookmaking bar owner in Kenosha named Angelo Salerno. He had joined the many thousands of the rest of us spread all over the United States.

John McEvoy
Evanston, Illinois 2001

CHAPTER 1

Vintage Year

How amazingly the planets aligned that spring morning in 1954 when within eight hours two of America's greatest racehorses first saw the light of day — in the very same foaling barn — at famed Claiborne Farm in central Kentucky.

The date such astronomical odds were defied was April 6. At 1:15 a.m. the mare Miss Disco dropped a dark bay Nasrullah colt. At 8:15 that morning, the mare Knight's Daughter foaled a bay son of Princequillo.

Bold Ruler was the first youngster to arrive that day. Bred by Mrs. Henry Carnegie Phipps' Wheatley Stable, he would go on to a wonderful racing career encompassing thirty-three starts, twenty-three wins, a three-year-old colt championship, and, in 1957, Horse of the Year honors gained in closely contested balloting. When he returned to his birthplace for stud duty, Bold

Ruler became an eight-time champion sire and undoubtedly would have dominated even longer had he not died prematurely.

Round Table was the second youngster to arrive that day at Claiborne Farm. He also was the same horse who narrowly lost the 1957 Horse of the Year title to Bold Ruler. He earned that crown the following year, though, and went back to his birthplace in 1960 as the world's leading money winner with $1,749,869 compiled during an incredible career that featured forty-three victories, more than one-third of them accomplished in record time. He, too, would earn leading sire status (1972) in a stud career that resulted in eighty-three stakes winners.

Bold Ruler was the more precocious and flashier of the two, turning in four record performances.

Round Table competed twice as many times as Bold Ruler but set or equaled three times as many track records. In his four-year career, the amazingly durable Round Table would make sixty-six starts, winning forty-three times (thirty-one in stakes) at distances from four furlongs to a mile and five-eighths, at fifteen different tracks across the United States. Five times, three of them while toting 130 pounds or more, Round Table blazed a mile and a quarter in less than 2:00. He set three American records, equaled one world record, set ten track records, and equaled another two — more record efforts than any other horse in American racing history.

This icon of diversity also won fourteen of his sixteen starts on the turf and became known as the finest grass horse ever produced in this country. Yet Round Table's record on dirt was also truly remarkable: his fifty starts on that surface produced twenty-nine victories and eleven records.

In the current age when trainers quail at the thought of handicap imposts exceeding 126 pounds, Round Table's weight-carrying capabilities border on the mythical: he picked up 130 pounds or more twenty-five times and won seventeen of them.

Despite his incredible racing record and reputation as one of the most tested weight carriers in the history of American racing, Round Table never enjoyed the media attention granted rival Bold Ruler. This was especially true in the East, probably because Bold Ruler was regarded as an "Eastern horse" owned by a member of racing's Establishment. There was a strong pro-Eastern bias in the racing press in those days.

Yet Round Table was not underappreciated. In the Midwest and California, where he did most of his racing, Round Table's appearances regularly attracted huge crowds. He was a Horse of the Year, a multiple champion, and a first-ballot Hall of Famer. He may not have "caught the fancy of the public" while performing as the favorite in most of his starts, but he was always held in high regard by racing people.

As the late *Blood-Horse* editor Kent Hollingsworth put it in 1984, "Of these two great colts, Round Table was always in a shadow while Bold Ruler was around. Bold Ruler was better early, Round Table was better longer, and richer...In the long run, Round Table was voted one of the 10 best horses to race in North America during the last half-century; and Bold Ruler was not."

Both Round Table and Bold Ruler are buried at Claiborne Farm, their legends continuing to shine brightly.

The U.S. Thoroughbred foal crop of 1954 is widely considered to be the best ever, rivaled perhaps only by the crop of 1928, which featured Equipoise, Twenty Grand, Mate, and Jamestown. The class of 1954 was even classier though — and deeper than an oil sheikh's pockets. In addition to Round Table and Bold Ruler, it included another eventual Hall of Famer, Gallant Man, as well as the stakes stars Iron Liege, Gen. Duke, Clem, Vertex, Federal Hill, Barbizon, One-Eyed King, Nashville, Cohoes, Amarullah, Promised Land, Missile, Better Bee, Greek Game, Ambehaving, Prince Khaled, Assemblyman, Lucky Mel, and King Hairan.

The superior nature of this crop was emphasized by the field for the 1957 Kentucky Derby: of the nine starters, no fewer than seven had already tied or broken track records in their young careers.

Emphasizing the class of the crop's top three — Round Table, Bold Ruler, and Gallant Man — was the fact each dominated older horses at age three and continued to beat the best at age four, with Round Table even going on to do so at age five.

It was further indication of harmonic convergences at work not only that Round Table was born at Claiborne on the same day as Bold Ruler, but also that he should have been born at all. The saga that resulted in his production had more twists and turns than a mountain stage in the Tour de France.

The most dramatic player in this drama was Round Table's sire, Princequillo, an equine refugee of World War II. This son of Prince Rose was, because of that conflict, conceived in France, foaled in England, reared in Ireland, and raced in the United States.

In 1932 an American businessman and Thoroughbred owner-breeder named L.L. "Laudy" Lawrence observed the Belgian champion Prince Rose, an English-bred son of Rose Prince, win impressively against other European stakes stars at Saint-Cloud racecourse in France. Lawrence subsequently bought a breeding farm in France, stocked it with well-bred mares, and bred several of them to Prince Rose, who was then at stud in Belgium and siring numerous winners in Europe.

Six years after being so impressed by Prince Rose at Saint-Cloud, the persistent Lawrence managed to lease the stallion for three years and brought him to his French farm Haras de Chefreville. In 1940 German troops occupied the farm and controlled the property until 1944 when American troops liberated it. An unfortunate victim of that skirmish was Prince Rose, who was killed in his stall by an American shell.

In 1939, one year before the Germans had moved

onto Haras de Chefreville, Lawrence had bred the stakes-winning mare Cosquilla to Prince Rose. Late that year, Lawrence sent Cosquilla across the English Channel to escape the German invasion, and it was in England that she foaled Princequillo in 1940. Not long after, the well-traveled Cosquilla and her suckling foal were shipped to Ireland.

With the war raging in Europe, Lawrence decided to send several of his yearlings — Princequillo among them — to the United States. Their trip by ship was not easy as the vessel had to make its way through waters of the North Atlantic that were infested by German U-boats.

After his horses had arrived in the United States, Lawrence made the decision to sell some of them. Princequillo was offered to an Argentine horse owner, who turned him down. Next, Lawrence attempted to sell the youngster to his friend Louis B. Mayer, the movie mogul whom Lawrence had helped enter racing as an owner and breeder. Again, the answer was no.

Finally, New Orleans sportsman Anthony Pelleteri, owner of Fair Grounds racecourse and a friend of Mayer's, agreed to lease Princequillo. After having bro-

ken his maiden going five and a half furlongs at Saratoga as a juvenile, Princequillo began to descend the class ladder, racing nine other times that 1942 season for claiming prices of $1,500 and $2,500. Pelleteri's lease allowed him to race Princequillo in claimers, and he did so at the risk of losing the horse. It was for $2,500 that trainer Horatio Luro haltered Princequillo for the Boone Hall Stable he operated in partnership with Princess Dimitri Djordjadze (the former Audrey Emory of Cincinnati, Ohio). Luro ran him for $3,500 with no takers; the "Gran Senor" then went on to develop Princequillo into one of the nation's top handicap horses.

Princequillo advanced from claiming events to allowance races to cup races. He beat the older Shut Out in the mile and a quarter Saratoga Handicap and won against the older Bolingbroke in the two-mile Jockey Club Gold Cup. According to the *American Racing Manual*, he was "generally regarded as the Cup champion of 1943." The next season he won the mile and three-sixteenths Merchants' and Citizens' Handicap, then tied a track record in taking the mile and five-eighths Questionnaire Handicap. He wound up winning twelve of his thirty-three career starts and $96,550 in purses.

Following his 1944 campaign, Princequillo was retired and entered stud at Arthur B. Hancock Sr.'s Ellerslie Farm in Virginia. When the Hancocks subsequently shifted their operation to Claiborne near Paris, Kentucky, Princequillo took up residence there as the property of a syndicate. This frequently displaced horse, bounced from country to country and owner to owner, had finally found a permanent home. At Claiborne Princequillo twice ranked as America's leading sire: in 1957, when his offspring compiled a then-record $1,698,427 (that mark lasted until 1966, when Bold Ruler broke it); and in 1958. In the latter year, Princequillo was represented not only by Horse of the Year Round Table but by the two-year-old filly champion Quill. Princequillo also sired another Horse of the Year, Hill Prince; the champion filly Misty Morn; and such other cracks as Dedicate, How, Dotted Line, and Third Brother.

Princequillo was the champion broodmare sire eight times, including five years in a row from 1966 to 1970. That he was salvaged from war-ravaged Europe to become one of the major influences on breeding in the United States was a stroke of amazingly good fortune indeed.

When he acquired Round Table's dam Knight's Daughter, Arthur B. "Bull" Hancock Jr., son of the Claiborne founder, was becoming a practiced hand at importing important breeding stock. In 1949 he had negotiated the importation of eventual four-time leading American sire Nasrullah, who during his stud career at Claiborne Farm sired ninety-eight stakes winners, including Bold Ruler and Nashua.

The same year he put together the purchase of Nasrullah, Hancock, on a visit to England, was shown Knight's Daughter by the Royal Stud manager, Captain Moore, at Newmarket. As Hancock later said, "I had just paid a lot of money for the Hyperion mare Hydrangea and had no notion of buying another...But I saw Knight's Daughter led out for the buyers' inspection, and I liked her immediately." Hancock paid slightly less than $11,000 for Knight's Daughter and shipped her to Kentucky.

A foal of 1941, Knight's Daughter was by Sir Cosmo out of Feola, by the top miler Friar Marcus. Feola was classic-placed on the racecourse (English Oaks) and produced four stakes winners, including English One Thousand Guineas heroine Hypericum.

Knight's Daughter, described by England's *Racing Post* as a "thickset, muscular and powerful sprinter type," made four starts at age two, winning three, including a minor stakes. This, despite the fact that, according to the *Post*, she had a set of "imperfect forelegs (somewhat upright, with poor joints)" and that off the racetrack she was "idle and of evil disposition."

All of Knight's Daughter's starts were five-furlong races at Newmarket. In her only loss, she split a pastern, an injury that led her trainer, Cecil Boyd-Rochfort, to retire her, although the effects of the war may have also influenced that decision.

Hancock was able to buy Knight's Daughter at a reasonable price primarily because she was by a sprinting sire and had won only sprints, and, therefore, she did not meet the Royal Stud's specified requirements for attempting to produce a classic winner. As it turned out, of course, Knight's Daughter's "sprinting blood" proved to be a perfect mix with that of stamina specialist Princequillo. (In 1984, on a tour of Kentucky,

Her Majesty Queen Elizabeth II amended her schedule so that she could visit Round Table at Claiborne.)

Hancock adeptly used the colt's parentage in coming up with the name Round Table. (Actually, the Claiborne product was not the first Round Table to roam America's racetracks. The original Round Table was a foal of 1931 bred by William Woodward's famed Belair Stud. He was a son of Sir Gallahad III—Priscilla Ruley. He raced ninety-seven times in the course of six years, winning eighteen races and earning a less-than-regal $17,140.)

As a youngster, Round Table was a "real handful," according to both Claiborne farm manager John Sosby and the farm's veterinarian, Colonel Floyd Sager. Recalled Sosby in a 1983 interview with racing writer Charles R. Koch: "Round Table was a tough one to handle. He broke away at least once from every man who tried to lead him. And he'd go running off with his shank flying in the wind."

Added Sager, "But he knew how to relax when he got to the track." Once settled in the racing milieu, Round Table would become known for his adaptability and calm disposition, traits he would evidence throughout the remainder of his long life.

CHAPTER 2

A Cut Below

A mere twenty-two and a half months after hitting the ground at Claiborne Farm, Round Table hit the racetrack for the first of his sixty-six career outings.

The date was February 24, 1956, the setting Hialeah Park. It was not an auspicious debut, but not a bad one either, although the fact that this eventual expert at the classic distances would strike out for glory by going a mere three furlongs might strike some as richly ironical.

Hialeah in the 1950s regularly carded these dashes for neophytes. This one, timed in :33 2/5, was captured by a now long forgotten runner named Myla. Round Table, saddled by trainer Moody Jolley and ridden by Steve Brooks in Claiborne Farm's colors, was bumped at the start but made up some ground late to finish fourth, beaten two lengths. He went off at the longest odds of his career: 14.50-1.

Round Table's debut marked the first of thirteen straight appearances with Brooks aboard. The rider would also reappear for another two in 1959.

Brooks was the son of an itinerant horse trader. He was born in the early 1920s in the back of a covered wagon outside the town of McCook, Nebraska. Introduced to riding when he helped his father to break wild horses they caught in Wyoming and Idaho, Brooks was riding in races at county fairs and in country match races by the time he was ten years old.

Young Brooks was introduced to Thoroughbred racing by an uncle and in 1937 began riding at the smaller tracks in the Midwest. His first victory at a recognized track came in 1938 at Shreveport, Louisiana. Three years later, the first of two consecutive seasons in which he was the leading rider in Illinois (he topped the standings at several Chicago meetings throughout the 1940s), Brooks won his first stakes, the Arlington Matron.

A powerfully built four-foot-eleven-and-a-half inches and 111 pounds, Brooks became renowned as one of the strongest and most active whip riders of his time.

It was in 1942 at the New Orleans Fair Grounds that Brooks first rode horses trained by Moody Jolley. The next year he piloted the Jolley-trained Riverland, a six-thousand-dollar purchase, to triumphs in the Dixie Handicap at Pimlico and the Excelsior Handicap at old Jamaica on Long Island. After a few years as contract rider for Calumet Farm — a period in which he rode such champions as Citation, Coaltown, Bewitch, and Two Lea and won the 1949 Kentucky Derby with that outfit's Ponder — Brooks returned to freelancing and revived his association with Jolley.

Jolley had an extensive and diverse dossier in racing. Born in Nashville, Tennessee, for many years a Turf stronghold, Jolley grew up across the road from old Cumberland Park racetrack and began galloping horses there when he was twelve. He subsequently became an exercise rider, a jockey, a jockey's valet, jockey's agent, trainer, owner, and breeder. It was Jolley who, acting for fellow Tennessean John L. Greer, picked Foolish Pleasure out of the 1973 Saratoga yearling sales for $20,000. Two years later, and trained by Moody's son LeRoy, Foolish Pleasure won the Kentucky Derby.

The tall, lean Jolley began training for Bull Hancock in 1953. During his six years with Claiborne, he developed the champion fillies Bayou and Doubledogdare,

plus a host of other stakes winners.

Round Table's debut had been against winners. Seven weeks later, Jolley entered him in a maiden special weight event at Keeneland. The neat-looking little colt had been training well, something that had not eluded the Kentucky hardboots who made him the 6-5 favorite in a field of eight. Brooks put him on the lead at once, and Round Table remained there, arriving two and a half lengths in front of runner-up Pandean. He was timed in a good :50 3/5 for the "about" four furlongs, barely more than a second off the track record.

This victory on April 14, 1956, was notable from two standpoints: it was the first of forty-seven races in which Round Table would be favored in his sixty-six-race career, and it marked one of only three times he would win on an off track.

Round Table made one more start at Keeneland that spring, posting the first of his thirty-one career stakes victories in the Lafayette on April 25. Performing on a fast racing strip this time, Round Table beat Jet Colonel by a half-length while coming within a fifth of a second of the track record for the "about" four-furlong distance (:49 2/5). Then it was off with the rest of the Claiborne string to Chicago, where Round Table would in subsequent seasons enjoy some of the greatest successes of his remarkable career. But he hardly set the world on fire that first summer at the Windy City area tracks.

Early leaders among the outstanding crop of 1954 were a pair of colts by the great speed influence sire Olympia. Greek Game, owned by Florida horseman Fred Hooper, who had raced Olympia, zipped undefeated through his first four starts. After breaking his maiden, he tacked on stakes victories in the Primer, Hyde Park, and Arlington Futurity.

While Greek Game was showing his heels to the cream of the Midwest juvenile crop, Mr. and Mrs. George Lewis' Lucky Mel was winning seven of eleven starts in California, including his last six in a row. Four of those wins came in stakes, and Lucky Mel set a then-world record of :56 3/5 for five furlongs in one of them, the Haggin. This West Coast speedball was trained by William "Bill" Molter, who less than a year later would take over the conditioning of Round Table.

After the Hollywood Park meeting closed, West met Midwest in the Prairie Stakes at old Washington Park in Chicago. For the first time, Greek Game was beaten

out of the gate — by Lucky Mel. However, that colt was run down by another invader, Rex Ellsworth's California Kid, who subsequently also finished first in the Washington Park Futurity but was disqualified and placed second behind Greek Game.

Neither Greek Game, Lucky Mel, nor California Kid won another stakes that season, and the 1956 two-year-old championship went to Calumet Farm's late-starting Barbizon, who didn't enter public life until September 15 but then reeled off four victories in six weeks. Barbizon's crown-clincher came in the rich Garden State Stakes, in which his eighteen victories included the heavily favored Bold Ruler (who finished seventeenth), Federal Hill (second, beaten a nose), plus Iron Liege and Clem, all of whom would play key roles in major three-year-old events the following year. (Barbizon, supposedly the victim of the "Garden State jinx" prevalent in those years, would never again approach his two-year-old form.)

Round Table, too, would be a powerful factor at three, although his 1956 Chicago campaign didn't produce any terribly strong indications of that. After Round Table took a June 28 allowance race, in which he downed Jet Colonel for the second straight time,

31

Jolley entered him right back in the Hyde Park Stakes on July 4. Round Table broke tardily, then closed well to be beaten five lengths by Greek Game in the five and a half-furlong race over a "good" Arlington Park strip.

Round Table next met Greek Game seventeen days later in the $140,000 Arlington Park Futurity. Again, the track was "off" — labeled sloppy this time — and Greek Game proved an easy winner after covering six furlongs in 1:12 1/5. Round Table got off to a better start that day, but gave up ground thereafter and arrived fourth. For Round Table, who liked to plant his feet firmly, slippery going was an anathema. (The colt's lone poor effort on grass was on a "soft" course.)

One more Chicago start remained on Round Table's schedule that summer. This came in a minor stakes, the $18,000 George Woolf Memorial, on the August 6 card at Washington Park. The normally sure-footed Round Table stumbled badly at the start. Brooks fell off — he was not injured — and Chicago fans' final view of Round Table that season was of a riderless horse. He and Brooks were booed by those who had made Round Table the 2.10-1 second choice in the race won by Smart Phil.

After four races in five weeks in Chicago, Jolley

gave Round Table more than a month off and returned him to Keeneland. Round Table returned to his winning ways, too, in an October 11 allowance race at six furlongs. After pressing the early pace, Round Table was a handy winner by a length and a half, flashing six furlongs in 1:10 1/5 to just miss tying the track record.

That good prep set Round Table up perfectly for Keeneland's premier two-year-old event, the $66,000 Breeders' Futurity at "about" seven furlongs on October 20.

Round Table took on nine rivals that day. Brooks employed different tactics, having his mount in seventh place through the first half-mile. He then put Round Table to a drive, and the Claiborne colt blew past Missile in the final fifty yards to win convincingly by a half-length, his final time in 1:26 4/5.

That clocking was again just two-fifths off the track standard, prompting Hancock to comment that Round Table had come "within one-fifth of a second of a track record each time (at Keeneland) that he caught a surface on which he could gain traction.

"He runs directly off his hocks," Round Table's breeder added.

Round Table's Breeders' Futurity score capped a sensationally successful meeting for the Claiborne Farm horses. The day before the Futurity, their three-year-old filly Doubledogdare won the inaugural running of the Spinster Stakes. All told, Jolley-trained horses owned by Claiborne made eleven starts at that fall Keeneland session and won six races.

Whether it was the different surface at Churchill Downs, or the effects of a rigorous juvenile campaign, Round Table performed dismally in his next and final start at two. It was a $7,500 allowance event on November 3, a mere two weeks after his Breeders' Futurity heroics. Jolley evidently wanted to get one more race out of Round Table before the stable shipped south. He didn't get much of one: at even money, Round Table barely got out of a high gallop. Racing wide all the way, he finished eighth behind Charlie's Song.

It was an uncharacteristic performance in a year that had seen Round Table win half of his ten starts. What was typical about the year was he ran at five different tracks. This renowned Thoroughbred commuter would eventually wind up running at a total of fifteen racetracks all over the continent. Not long after his

dismal Churchill Downs effort, Round Table ran a nail through one of his feet and was given a respite.

In the Experimental Free Handicap for two-year-olds of 1956, Round Table was assigned 118 pounds, as were five others: Lucky Mel, California Kid, Nashville, Mister Jive, and Melson. Nine rivals were rated above Round Table and his poundage peers. The highweight at 126 pounds was champion Barbizon, followed by Bold Ruler and Federal Hill, both at 125; Greek Game, Amarullah, Ambehaving, and King Hairan, all at 122; and Prince Khaled and Missile, both at 120.

Although he had won a pair of stakes races and earned $73,326, Round Table was obviously considered to be a cut below the cream of his crop. Bold Ruler banked $139,050 that season, but Greek Game — who would never again win a stakes — wound up as the two-year-old money leader with $214,805.

But that would all change, as would so many other things in Round Table's life as the result of events that unfolded under the Florida sun in early 1957.

CHAPTER 3

Well Sold, Well Bought

A s the horses warmed up before him for the fifth race at Hialeah Park on the afternoon of February 9, 1957, Dr. John Peters later admitted he had been "very nervous." And he had good reason to be. He was under pressure to decide whether to spend a considerable amount of another man's money for a horse that had finished tenth, beaten ten lengths by Gallant Man, in his seasonal debut three weeks earlier in the Hibiscus Stakes.

Bull Hancock, with whom Peters was sitting in a clubhouse box at Hialeah that day, also was feeling pressure. With his father's health failing — Arthur B. Hancock would pass away three weeks later — Bull was now the master of famed Claiborne Farm, one of America's great breeding establishments, but one with serious estate tax burdens looming.

The senior Hancock had built Claiborne into a major commercial breeding operation that ranked as America's leader in races won for nine years. But in 1945 Hancock developed serious heart trouble. His son Bull, at that time a captain in the U.S. Army, was released from active duty to return home and assume responsibility for running Claiborne.

That February afternoon at Hialeah these two men — the veterinarian from the West Coast and the veteran horseman from the Bluegrass — were about to finalize one of the most significant horse sales in history. Changing hands would be Round Table, the eventual world's leading money-winning racehorse.

In Oklahoma at the beginning of 1957 lived a man who had a fervent desire to own a classic contender — and the wherewithal to afford one. Travis Mitchell Kerr, born in Ada, Oklahoma, in 1902, began his business career selling oil-field equipment in the Sooner State and Texas. After his brother Robert S. Kerr, who was to become a powerful U.S. senator, co-founded an oil drilling company in 1929, Travis joined its management team and eventually served as vice-chairman of the board of the giant Kerr-McGee Oil Industries.

Travis Kerr had gotten hooked on horse racing when friends took him to Washington Park during a visit to Chicago to see a football game. In subsequent years Kerr, his wife, Geraldine (Jerry), and their daughter, Nancy (later Mrs. Cecil Magana), frequently attended races at the California tracks when visiting there. In 1948 Kerr joined in a small syndicate that campaigned a few cheap horses. When that stable was dissolved, Kerr, now avidly interested in the sport, bought three broodmares. From this small band emerged three stakes-caliber horses: Breezing Bebe, Ole Travis, and Lover Boy. All were developed for Kerr by R.H. "Red" McDaniel, the five-time (1950-54) national leading trainer in races won.

On May 5, 1955, the forty-four-year-old McDaniel committed suicide by jumping off the San Francisco Bay Bridge only minutes after saddling a winner at nearby Golden Gate Fields. While the shock of this tragedy was still wearing off, Kerr began looking for a new trainer. His search went no further than an adjacent clubhouse box at Hollywood Park belonging to William "Bill" Molter. He was the trainer of 1954 Kentucky Derby winner Determine and many other stakes stars, including On Trust (a winner of $554,145). Molter also was the

man whom McDaniel edged out for the national training title in the final week of the 1952 season.

This relationship got off to an auspicious start in the
summer of 1955 when Kerr purchased New York sprint
star Bobby Brocato for $150,000. Displaying patience
and persistence, Molter managed to harness Bobby
Brocato's speed and convert him into a fine distance
performer. "When we first got Bobby Brocato, we
couldn't work him five furlongs in more than :58 or :59
without hampering him with too tight a hold. But later
he would work in 1:04 or even slower if asked to,"
Molter once said.

This conversion of talents was, before his work with
Round Table, Molter's major achievement in horseman-
ship. Bobby Brocato ranked second only to the great
Swaps among West Coast handicap horses and retired
with earnings of $504,510. He earned the bulk of that
sum while racing for Kerr.

Kerr also raced such good ones as Prince Blessed, a
$77,000 yearling purchase who went on to earn
$255,805; and Demobilize, a stakes winner of $168,961.
(Prince Blessed, a younger stablemate of Round Table,
later had a stud career distinguished primarily by his sir-

ing of Ole Bob Bowers, who would, in turn, sire two-time Horse of the Year John Henry.) Kerr's Thoroughbred holdings — racing and breeding stock — eventually swelled to more than 110 head. Kerr bred his first winner in 1955, and he and his wife and daughter bred several dozen more winners thereafter.

Kerr had met Peters, a respected veterinarian, in California. He employed Peters to scout for horses to buy. Also serving Kerr in that capacity was the multifaceted Joe Hernandez, a longtime track announcer (the "voice of Santa Anita") who owned horses himself and operated a bloodstock agency. Both men played major roles in Kerr's acquisition of Round Table.

As a bloodstock agent, Hernandez for years had dealt with Claiborne, which each year sent horse brokers a list of stock available for purchase. Appearing on that list in 1956 was the two-year-old Round Table, initially priced at $40,000 by Bull Hancock. Hernandez observed Round Table in workouts at Keeneland that spring. He recommended Kerr buy what Hernandez described as this "smallish, quiet youngster." Kerr was interested, but Molter advised him that the price was too high for a maiden.

Round Table broke his maiden at Keeneland and then won his stakes debut there. Shipped to Chicago, the colt won an allowance race and finished second in the Hyde Park Stakes. Bull Hancock told Hernandez the price had gone up — to $60,000. Again, Kerr demurred.

After Round Table stretched out in distance and captured the Breeders' Futurity at Keeneland that fall, Hancock bumped the asking price to $125,000. He also insisted that he retain twenty percent of the colt when Round Table eventually went to stud. Despite the escalation in asking price, Kerr remained interested. Furthermore, Kerr's wife and daughter were pushing for the purchase because they were "fascinated" with the colt's name.

Like Hernandez, Peters had been scouring the nation's backstretches looking for horses that Kerr might buy. He spent a great deal of time at Hialeah, for there was a wealth of talent stabled there, including Bold Ruler, Iron Liege, Gen. Duke, and Gallant Man; but none of that quartet was for sale. At one point that winter, Peters arranged for Kerr to buy the good three-year-old Federal Hill. However, Federal Hill suffered a minor injury and the deal fell through.

Visiting Moody Jolley's barn one morning, Peters inquired about prospects. Jolley told him, "Everything in the barn is for sale." When Peters said he was looking for a three-year-old colt, Jolley replied, "The little one out front is the best one we've got." It was Round Table. After looking him over, Peters reported to Kerr that Round Table was "the soundest looking colt you ever saw."

On February 6, 1957, a deal was struck between Hancock and Kerr. Over the years the sale price has variously been reported as $140,000 and $145,000 and "about $150,000" and, more often, $175,000. Taking into account the commissions paid by Kerr, the latter figure probably most accurately describes the deal.

As Hernandez put it, "Mr. Kerr never did back off, even when the price was going up like an express elevator." The money was transferred that day to the Tobacco Farmers National Bank of Paris, Kentucky, from the First National Bank of Oklahoma City. All that remained was for veterinarian Peters to give his stamp of approval.

Peters was in California the day the money was transferred. Hurriedly, he arranged to fly to Florida to

make his final appraisal of Round Table, who was entered in the fifth race at Hialeah on Saturday. Molter had intended to accompany Peters but had to settle for a different flight, one that was later grounded in Kansas City because of bad weather. The day of the race Peters flew into Tampa at 1 p.m. and then took a plane to Miami where he had arranged for a car to rush him to the racetrack.

When Peters strode into the Hialeah paddock as the horses were being saddled for the fifth, Hancock said, "Where you been? You got to buy this horse before he runs today, or the deal's off."

Hancock handed his binoculars to Peters so that the veterinarian could watch Round Table on his way to the post. Peters asked how long he had to decide whether to okay the deal. "Until that bell rings," Hancock replied. As the little bay walked into his stall in the gate, Peters nodded in the affirmative, and the two men shook hands on the deal. At that moment the bell rang for the race's start.

Racing in the middle of the track most of the way, Round Table finished sixth. A concerned Peters sought out jockey Steve Brooks after the race. "You can throw the race out," Brooks said, adding: "He lost more ground on the two turns than he was beat (eleven lengths by eventual Kentucky Derby winner Iron Liege). You got a good colt. He'll win a lot of races," Brooks assured Peters.

When Peters reported to Kerr by phone, the Oklahoman commented, "it was a lot of money to pay for a horse that beat only one other." But he told Peters "not to worry." When Molter finally arrived at Hialeah the next day, he pronounced himself pleased with Round Table's appearance.

The colt's "appearance" then was in a 960-pound package, one that would increase by some fifty pounds that spring and not much more after that. Round Table throughout his life was a good "doer," but he would never tilt the scales.

Describing Round Table in 1958, Peters said: "Round Table is slightly over at the knee and in stride has a rolling motion, with the leg bent a little as it takes his weight. As Bull has said, Round Table runs off his hocks. He has no bad habits and is so kind and gentle a two-year-old kid can walk him. He's as sound now as when we got him, not a pimple on him.

"One thing that first caught my eye," Peters continued, "was his walk. Round Table overstrides by about a foot, and I remembered hearing for a long time that when a horse put his hind foot down in front of the print of the forefoot, it was a sign he was a good one."

In addition to retaining a twenty percent interest in Round Table as a stallion, Bull Hancock by means of this deal secured Claiborne's future. As Hancock put it, the sale "more or less held the farm together, paid the estate taxes, and so on," after the death of his father.

Years later, Hancock commented of the transaction, "I was crazy about Round Table and wanted to keep him. I had three Princequillo colts that year. I priced Round Table at $40,000 and the other two at $20,000 each. Everybody came and looked at Round Table, and everybody passed him by."

When he took over the handling of Round Table in the winter of 1957, forty-seven-year-old Bill Molter was one of America's most successful horsemen. He was practiced not only at winning races in bunches but also in preparing stakes-class runners to do their best. His ability to first lead his peers in total wins and then go on to top them in money won was rare, manifested by only a handful of American horsemen.

Born in 1910 (1911 or 1912, according to some reports) in Fredericksburg, Texas, the same town that produced Hall of Fame trainer Max Hirsch, Molter was the son of a rancher and thus exposed to horses from an early age. Fredericksburg had a half-mile training track that was in use throughout the year. Molter began riding in Quarter Horse races there before he turned twelve.

As a teenager, Molter branched out into Thoroughbred race riding at bush tracks and county fairs before linking up with legendary trainer Preston Burch as a groom and then exercise rider. (Burch, elected to the Hall of Fame in 1963, authored the classic *Training Thoroughbred Horses*, still in print today.)

After riding in Mexico (he had several mounts on the memorable program of March 20, 1932 — the day the great Phar Lap won the Caliente Handicap in sensational style), western Canada, and northern California, Molter was forced to retire from the saddle in 1934 due to increasing weight. He immediately turned to training and sent out his first winner, Holmfirth, at Caliente on March 3, 1935, while working as an assistant to L.O. Lee, trainer of the prominent Jack P. Atkin stable. In 1939 Molter put together a small public stable based in Los Angeles. The racing blackout on the West Coast during World War II led him to New York and Chicago tracks.

Molter was the leading trainer in winners from 1946 through 1949 (he tied with Midwest powerhouse William Hal Bishop the latter year). During much of that decade, Molter competed directly with Red McDaniel.

It was as an offshoot of the amazing success of Molter, McDaniel, and other trainers of public stables in the West that the "stablemate" rule was introduced into American racing. (To combat these training colossi, the California Racing Board at one time passed a rule limiting to forty the maximum number of horses any one trainer could have on the grounds.)

After his tenure as leading trainer in winners, Molter — much in the manner of his New York-based counterpart Hirsch Jacobs — set his sights on the money title. He succeeded. Molter led all trainers in money won in 1954, 1956, 1958, and 1959. Besides Round Table, other stable stars in that period included 1954 Kentucky Derby winner Determine, owned by Andrew Crevolin, and Bobby Brocato and Imbros. (Seven years before Determine's score, Molter became the first trainer to fly a major contender to the Kentucky Derby when he sent On Trust from California to Louisville, where the colt finished fourth.)

The soft-spoken, hard-working Molter was highly regarded by his contemporaries both for his talents as a horseman and for his gracious personality. He was well known for his extreme reluctance to advise friends, or even his owners, on whether to bet one of his charges. Molter once told San Francisco racing writer Abe Kemp, "It just hurts me inside when a friend of mine loses money on my horses. It makes me sick."

One week after trailing Iron Liege home by eleven somewhat disheartening lengths, Round Table made his final start of the 1957 Florida winter season. Saddled by Moody Jolley for the final time, and carrying Travis Kerr's Kelly green and chartreuse colors for the first time, Round Table took on a field of eight rivals in a seven-furlong allowance event. Under Steve Brooks, Round Table dashed directly to the front with an opening quarter in :22 4/5. He led by six lengths the remainder of the way, posting excellent fractions of :45 1/5 and 1:09 2/5 en route to a final clocking of 1:22 2/5, which was just two-fifths off the Hialeah track record.

Any gust of air felt at Hialeah that afternoon might have represented the collective sigh of relief emanating from Kerr, Peters, Hernandez, and Hancock, for Round Table had strongly indicated that he was both well sold and well bought.

And there were many, many much better days ahead.

ROUND TABLE

CHAPTER 4

Signs Of Greatness

It's a long way from South Florida to Southern California, and a long way from a $5,000 allowance race to the $98,000 Santa Anita Derby. Yet it was at the Arcadia track and in the Santa Anita Derby that Round Table appeared on the afternoon of March 2, 1957, only three weeks after he had become the property of Travis M. Kerr. Thus began what racing writer Carter Swart once described as "the finest three years of equine barnstorming ever seen in America." It also marked the third of what would become an astounding fourteen straight months of competition for the hardy little colt.

The mile and one-eighth Santa Anita Derby would be the first of nineteen starts for Round Table in the Golden State over the next two years. He would win thirteen of those starts, but not this first one.

Competing on a "slow" track, Round Table went to the front at the furlong pole but couldn't hold his lead and finished third behind the winner Sir William, beaten a head and a nose. This was Round Table's first photo finish, and he lost it at level weights (118 pounds). His sixty-six-race career would include nine more photo finishes, seven of which he would win. His two photo-finish defeats saw him giving away seventeen and twenty-one pounds to the horses that edged him out.

Round Table's next race was a bigger disappointment, for he finished a well-beaten fifth in the San Bernardino Handicap on March 11. Again, the track was "off," being labeled "muddy." Molter began to suspect that Round Table heartily disliked such going, that he was uncomfortable on such surfaces and unwilling to extend himself over them. It would be seventeen months and thirty races (twenty-five of them winning efforts) later before Round Table would again finish out of the money.

Sent north, Round Table relished his return to a fast racing strip with a win in the Bay Meadows Derby on April 6. Ridden by Ralph Neves ("The Portuguese Pepperpot") for the first of five straight races, Round Table covered the mile and one-sixteenth in 1:41 3/5, the fastest time for the distance by a three-year-old in Bay Meadows' history, despite being eased up near the wire.

This performance encouraged the Kerrs to start "thinking Kentucky Derby." The Kerrs had never had a Derby starter, and both Jerry and Nancy were enthusiastic about taking Round Table east. So was Neves, who praised Round Table as definitely being of "Derby caliber." Molter did not share their enthusiasm, aware that Bold Ruler and Calumet Farm's Gen. Duke had been beating each other in record times in the major Florida stakes, and that Gallant Man was of that high caliber, too.

Kerr insisted that he wouldn't do anything unless Molter gave the go-ahead. In turn, Molter said, "It's all up to Mr. Kerr." The Kerrs were undoubtedly aware that the conservative Molter had not wanted to send Determine from California to Louisville three years earlier, believing the Derby was too demanding a race for young three-year-olds. Molter had been overruled by Andrew Crevolin, Determine's owner, and found himself in the Churchill winner's circle following the Run for the Roses.

(In 1954 Molter accompanied Determine on the flight to Louisville from San Francisco. When the trainer boarded the cargo plane, he was handed a revolver by one of the pilots. Molter asked what the gun was for. "Why, to shoot the horse if he goes berserk in midair and endangers the plane," he was told. Molter handed the gun back to the pilot, saying, "I'd shoot myself first before I would do anything to Determine.")

The Kerr family debate lasted about twenty-four hours. Finally, Travis declared Round Table would return to Kentucky. The Oklahoma oilman's deep involvement with his avocation was becoming well known by this time. According to a *Daily Racing Form* story, "Few owners, if any, are seen more often around the stable area in the mornings than Kerr. He knows every one of his horses with the accuracy of a first-rate clocker. He can be away from a weanling or yearling for several months during its growing period, but he'll seldom be stumped. He has a wonderful eye for conformation and his knowledge of bloodlines is only behind his interest, which is insatiable. 'Teak' and his family are a major factor in major racing in America."

Before shipping, Round Table worked a mile in

1:36 2/5 at Bay Meadows. Back on his native soil he turned in another blistering drill: six furlongs in 1:09 4/5 preparing for the April 25 Blue Grass Stakes (the Keeneland race for many years was run on the Thursday of pre-Derby week).

Round Table ran back to his recent good workouts in the Blue Grass, which carried a purse of just $31,000. A crowd of 8,450 turned out under cloudy skies and watched Neves usher the even-money favorite through the first three-quarters of a mile on a dawdling lead. At the head of the stretch, the field bunched up. A few taps of the whip by Neves followed, and Round Table detached himself to score by six widening lengths. His time of 1:47 2/5 shattered Correspondent's four-year-old track record of 1:49 for the nine furlongs.

Did Round Table like Keeneland? Well, he made five starts there and never lost. *The Blood-Horse* referred to him as "Keeneland's Lad."

Runner-up One-Eyed King was declared out of the Derby after this race. Kerr was overjoyed at Round Table's performance. "I hate to say so but I think he is better than Bobby Brocato, my favorite horse, up to now," Kerr commented.

Less impressed was jockey Bill Hartack, who rode One-Eyed King in the Blue Grass, but who was the regular pilot of pre-Derby favorite Gen. Duke. Said Hartack, "I thought I had the best Derby horse (Gen. Duke) before the race, and I still think I have the best Derby horse."

Hartack had his reasons. Gen. Duke had enjoyed a brilliant Florida campaign. He beat Bold Ruler by a head in the Everglades Stakes at Hialeah in track-record time of 1:47 2/5 for a mile and one-eighth, lost to Bold Ruler by a neck in the Flamingo, then downed Bold Ruler by a convincing length and a half in Gulfstream Park's Florida Derby, equaling a world record of 1:46 4/5 for the nine furlongs. Sadly, Gen. Duke went lame at Churchill Downs and was scratched from the Derby field on the morning of the race. He never raced again and had to be put down the following year when a neurological disease caused him to lose his coordination.

Even in the absence of Gen. Duke, the 1957 Kentucky Derby field ranks as probably the greatest ever. Record-setting members of the nine-horse field included not only Round Table but Bold Ruler, Federal

Hill, and Iron Liege, who carried the Calumet Farm hopes in Gen. Duke's absence. No fewer than three of the contestants — Round Table, Bold Ruler, and Gallant Man — would wind up in the Hall of Fame.

This was the first Kentucky Derby the Kerr family had ever attended and the first in which Ralph Neves had ridden. It proved to be a dissatisfying occasion for all of them. Iron Liege won under Hartack as Bill Shoemaker, aboard Gallant Man, misjudged the finish line to miss by a nose. Round Table finished third, nearly three lengths behind Iron Liege and three lengths in front of Bold Ruler.

Bull Hancock was not deeply discouraged. "Round Table was in a switch about the five-sixteenths pole, and I thought he ran very well over that cuppy track. Every time we ran him at two and he caught his (fast) racetrack, he was within a fifth of a second of the track record. As I've said, he runs right off his hocks, and I think it scares him when he hits a soft, shifty racetrack." (The track that day was officially rated as "fast.")

While Bold Ruler went on to win the Preakness and Gallant Man the Belmont Stakes, Round Table was returned to California. Said Jerry Kerr, "After he lost

the Derby, it never occurred to us to run him in those other races (classics)."

Things did not turn around immediately for Round Table back on the West Coast. Three weeks after the Derby, Round Table ran second in Hollywood Park's Californian — beaten by Social Climber in Round Table's first attempt against older horses. Then came a memorable reversal of fortune and form.

Only five days later, Round Table made his third start of the month. In the May 30 Will Rogers Stakes at Hollywood, facing fellow three-year-olds, Round Table carried Neves to a three-and-a-half-length tally over Joe Price, his mile in a brisk 1:34 2/5 under 122 pounds.

The Will Rogers started an eleven-race winning streak for Round Table, the longest compiled by a three-year-old since Citation in 1948. All the races were at distances between a mile and a mile and a quarter — his preferred parameters as his overall career would establish. (After the win skein came to a halt, the redoubtable Round Table, thriving on as demanding a schedule as any trainer has ever devised for a great horse, launched another win skein that eventually reached eight. In fact, starting with the Will Rogers, Round Table won twenty-two of twenty-four races.)

Of the eleven-race win streak, Joe A. Estes, writing in *American Race Horses for 1957*, noted, "There was to be a singular uniformity about these races, as if the colt could be wound up like a toy and go through the same routine whenever his trainer pleased. Round Table was always either in front or close behind the leaders in the early running. Usually he was being eased before the finish was reached, usually carrying top weight and always, when there was betting, he was the favorite."

(Estes was referring to only the 1957 season, but his comments could apply with equal accuracy to Round Table's four- and five-year-old campaigns.)

Slightly more than two weeks later, Round Table took the El Dorado Handicap at Hollywood under jockey George Taniguchi. Round Table had given Joe Price four pounds in the Will Rogers to win by three and a half; this time, he conceded eleven pounds to Joe Price, yet won by an even larger margin, seven lengths, covering the mile and one-sixteenth in 1:41.

Although Taniguchi was under contract to the Kerr Stables, a disagreement ruptured this alliance, and the

El Dorado turned out to be his lone appearance aboard the Kerr colt, just as Eddie Arcaro, Hartack, and P.J. Bailey had only ridden him once. Ismael "Milo" Valenzuela rode Round Table twice, Longden three times, Bill Harmatz four times, Neves five times, and Brooks fifteen times.

But starting with the Cinema Handicap on July 6, 1957, Round Table would join forces with a man with whom he would enter the starting gate an amazing thirty-three times: Bill Shoemaker. Their partnership would result in twenty-six victories, three seconds, two thirds, and two unplaced finishes.

Shoemaker, born in Fabens, Texas, on August 19, 1931, never rode a horse during his early years in the Lone Star State. As *Daily Racing Form*'s Leon Rasmussen wrote in 1950, "Shoemaker's parents separated and were divorced 'when I was so small I don't remember,' he says. Both were born in Texas. His father, Shoemaker says, 'is Irish' and his mother 'mostly Dutch.' Until the boy was ten, Shoemaker's dad worked in a cottonseed mill at Fabens but, with the outbreak of World War II, came to Los Angeles to work in one of the aircraft factories. Willie came West with his dad and went to grade school and spent 'a little' high school time in El Monte.

"It was while he was at El Monte High School he finally got the start he wanted. He hooked on at the Suzy Q Ranch of Thomas W. Simmons, an owner, breeder and one of the founders of Hollywood Park. He was sixteen. He stayed there a year, mucking out stalls and breaking yearlings. It was at Suzy Q that 'I learned how to stay on a horse,' he says."

(Ironically, Shoemaker as a youth had no intentions of becoming a jockey. As he told another *Daily Racing Form* writer, Mike Marten, in 1981: "I was in high school and a girl in one of my classes was dating a jockey. She introduced me to him and he got me a job on the Suzy Q ranch. Things just went from there.")

After turning seventeen, Shoemaker felt he was ready for the next step, one that would take him from the ranch to the racetrack. He first went to Bay Meadows, where he got work as an exercise rider for the stable of Charles S. Howard (of Seabiscuit fame), whose trainer then was Hurst Philpot.

In addition to being a natural talent, Shoemaker was a natural lightweight, standing four-foot-eleven and weigh-

ing 102 pounds. For many years after that, Shoemaker weighed between ninety-seven and one hundred pounds.

Shoemaker won his first race aboard Shafter V at Golden Gate Fields in 1949 — the first entry in a career that completely rewrote the jockey record book over the next forty years. He led the nation in money won ten times (including a record seven in a row from 1958 through '64) and races won five times. He won four Kentucky Derbys (the last at age fifty-four in 1986 on Ferdinand, becoming the oldest jockey to win the classic), five Belmonts, and the Preakness Stakes.

His mounts over the years included, in addition to Round Table and Gallant Man, such Hall of Famers as Spectacular Bid, John Henry, Swaps, Buckpasser, Damascus, Ack Ack, Bowl of Flowers, Cicada, Dahlia, Gun Bow, Northern Dancer, Native Diver, and Exceller.

In sharp contrast to "strongman" Steve Brooks, his predecessor as Round Table's regular rider, Shoemaker used the whip sparingly. He was the epitome of the sit-still, finesse rider, but could get horses to finish for him — or do most anything, for that matter. "Horses run for him" and "he has the greatest hands of any rider" were the two most common descriptions of the tiny Texan.

One of the best descriptions of Shoemaker was supplied in 1970 by Eddie Read, a veteran racing man and, at the time, Del Mar's assistant general manager.

Read told *Sports Illustrated*: Shoemaker is "cool, calm, all guts. He'll do absolutely nothing to a horse if that's what's called for, or he'll send a horse through a suicidal hole if that's what's called for. Fire and ice, that's it.

"He has an uncanny ability for positioning himself in a race," Read continued. "He's the master of the whole situation, and yet never seems to be doing anything up there. He doesn't scrub and rub around on a horse, like some of the jocks.

"He's like a little computer, sitting up there, knowing exactly when to do what, and moving the horse with little clucks and touches…Riding like that, Shoe doesn't take much out of a horse."

(In 1975 Shoemaker participated in a series of tests devised by Dr. Robert Kerlan, the prominent California surgeon and sports physician. The goal was to measure the physical fitness of athletes, and a number of football, baseball, basketball, and hockey players were involved. Kerlan established that Shoemaker, at age forty-four, was the fittest of them all. He weighed ninety-seven

pounds at the time, often playing several hours of tennis after riding five or six mounts in the afternoon.)

Molter appreciated Shoemaker's talents and riding style so much that, once their association began, he used him on Round Table every chance he had.

Shoemaker's introduction to Round Table in the Cinema Handicap resulted in a four-length score over — who else? — Joe Price. The weight spread this time was sixteen pounds as Round Table picked up 130 for the first time. Round Table covered the nine furlongs at Hollywood Park in 1:47 4/5.

If the competition in his previous three outings could be considered moderate, the field he next faced was anything but. And Round Table's performance served to stamp him as something very special, in the eyes of both the public and his jockey.

On July 13, 1957, before a record Hollywood Gold Cup Day crowd of 55,488, Round Table took on older horses going a mile and a quarter in the feature race. Favored at 7-5, he was facing some good ones, too: Porterhouse and Find, for example. These were quality handicappers and he blitzed them.

Carrying a comparative "feather" of 109 pounds,

Round Table blazed the mile and a quarter in 1:58 3/5, the fastest ten furlongs ever turned in by a three-year-old in the United States. The time also tied the great Swaps' track record (set when Swaps was four in 1956). Round Table's fractions were :45 2/5 for the half-mile, 1:09 1/5 for six furlongs, and 1:33 4/5 for the mile. Porterhouse trailed him home by more than three lengths, Find by another two, and Eddie Schmidt by nine as Round Table became the first three-year-old to win in the eighteen-year history of the Gold Cup, one of the West's premier prizes with its purse of $162,100. No other three-year-old had beaten older horses that early in the year at the Gold Cup distance in at least ten years. (Citation downed his elders going nine furlongs in the 1948 Stars and Stripes Handicap at Arlington in July, and Swaps in June of 1955 defeated older horses in the mile and one-sixteenth Californian.)

Shoemaker told newsmen after the Gold Cup, "Round Table is great, no mistake about that. We could have opened up on them at any time, because he was just galloping to the half-mile pole...I didn't ask him to do any running until we reached the quarter pole.

Then he was pricking his ears, so I shook him up a little bit. That was all."

Added Johnny Longden, rider of runner-up Porterhouse: "Round Table is one of the very best three-year-olds I ever saw."

Discussing Round Table in a 2001 interview, Shoemaker noted, "he was a real speed horse early on when I started riding him. Later on he got to where he didn't have to be on the lead."

ROUND TABLE

CHAPTER 5

Sensational Season

T he Hollywood Gold Cup purse of $100,000 brought Round Table's earnings for the year to $258,925, all of it gleaned since Kerr purchased the colt.

This sum would look fairly paltry in the seasons ahead, during which Round Table continued his inexorable march toward the title of the world's leading money-winning Thoroughbred. Still, his earnings and his Gold Cup tour de force combined to increase his value.

Prior to the Gold Cup, a prominent owner approached Peters about buying Round Table. Peters relayed this to Kerr, who said, "Well, I wouldn't take $999,999 for him, but a million will close the deal."

It didn't happen, and the Gold Cup clinched Kerr's determination to retain Round Table. Kerr told Peters, "He's not for sale at any price."

Molter by this time was having Round Table guarded like the crown jewels. Describing the horse's Hollywood accommodations, Molter said, "We keep him in a screened stall, padlocked. Only the foreman and groom have keys. There's a day watchman and night watchman. Round Table doesn't even have a chance to get lonesome."

When Kerr was asked whether Round Table would be gunning for Belmont Stakes winner Gallant Man, he responded: "We won't dodge Gallant Man or hunt for him. We'll just go in whatever races Molter decides. Whether Gallant Man's in them or out of them won't make any difference."

In his 1957 farewell to Hollywood Park, Round Table easily annexed the Westerner Stakes on July 20. Shortly thereafter, Molter's stable shipped to Chicago. The primary objective for Round Table was the rich American Derby on the Washington Park grass course August 31. Since the son of Princequillo had never competed over that surface, Washington Park management arranged a betless exhibition race on August 20. With Shoemaker sitting chilly, Round Table won smoothly from just off the pace, establishing to Molter's satisfaction that the colt "could handle grass."

Could he ever! In the $145,000 American Derby, Round Table showed his heels to Kentucky Derby hero Iron Liege, winning by four lengths in front-running fashion. He was timed in 1:55 for the mile and three-sixteenths, two-fifths of a second over the track standard. This was the first time longtime Chicago track executive William Thayer viewed Round Table in action. "I saw him many times after that," Thayer said in 2001, "and believe me, there was no better grass horse than Round Table. He could carry the grandstand and win."

Round Table totaled nineteen starts at Arlington Park, Washington Park, and Hawthorne Race Course in the next two and a half years. Of his fifteen victories at the three tracks, ten came in stakes.

Following the American Derby, the rivalry between Round Table and Gallant Man began to heat up again — at least in the press.

On September 4, *Daily Racing Form* columnist Charles Hatton wrote that "the onus of repudiating the everlasting form of the Kentucky Derby, in which Gallant Man came from behind and beat him decisive lengths, is on Round Table. He must come to Gallant Man."

Kerr took strong exception to this. The following day, he told the *Form*'s Oscar Otis that while he had "much respect for Hatton's judgment," he could not "follow his reasoning. Why should we have to go anywhere to prove anything. And why must we go to New York?

"I've said right along that nothing would please us better than to meet Gallant Man on a neutral ground," Kerr went on, "and by that I mean on a track that is fair to both horses.

"Our plans were announced well in advance, first the American Derby…then the United Nations. Gallant Man was eligible for the American Derby, but did not elect to start. Gallant Man was also invited to the United Nations, but declined." (Gallant Man never did run on the grass.)

Atlantic City management then proposed a match race, conditions to be agreed upon, but it never came off. Kerr's comments obviously nettled John Nerud, Gallant Man's trainer. Nerud said it had been made clear all along that Gallant Man would start next in the September 28 Woodward at Belmont Park. Kerr's remarks "don't call for any statement," said Nerud. Gallant Man did next run in the Woodward, finishing second to the older Dedicate, with Bold Ruler third.

In the American Derby and Hollywood Gold Cup, Round Table had displayed his brilliance. In the $100,000 United Nations Handicap at Atlantic City on September 14, he displayed his grit.

The eleven-horse line-up for the United Nations was solid. In addition to Round Table, who was assigned 118 pounds and favored at 7-10 despite taking on older horses and making only his third start on grass, it included the top-class Tudor Era as well as Hollywood Gold Cup third-place finisher Find.

When the field was dispatched for this mile and three-sixteenths test, Round Table stumbled and lost position. Shoemaker quickly gathered him together, and they soon engaged in a battle for the lead with Tudor Era, who was giving Round Table six pounds. At the end of an eventful stretch duel, Round Table prevailed by a nose over Tudor Era. Two lengths back came Find, who was two in front of Career Boy, winner of the United Nations the previous year.

The United Nations took twenty minutes to decide, for jockey Bobby Martin, aboard Tudor Era, claimed foul against Round Table, alleging bumping during the

stretch tussle. The stewards finally adjudged both horses equally at fault for the contact and let the result
stand. It was the eighth victory in a row for the horse
described in the Associated Press account as "the tiny
package of TNT."

This race highlighted two of Round Table's greatest
strengths: his athleticism and competitiveness. As Peters
said of him, "Round Table's a real athlete. He has stumbled leaving the gate, been knocked down and side-
ways, yet has never come back cut up. He's agile and
intelligent enough to protect himself."

The United Nations was one of five photo finishes
Shoemaker won aboard Round Table (he lost just one).
Shoemaker commented in 2001: "Round Table ran
with his head down and stretched out. Some horses
carry their heads high, but he wasn't one of them.
John Henry (whom Shoemaker rode years later) also
ran with his head down. I think that factor helped
them both to win close races — plus the fact that they
were mighty determined competitors."

Round Table was returned to Chicago after the
United Nations, his next goal the $126,000 Hawthorne
Gold Cup on October 12. Molter wanted to follow his

usual practice of giving the colt a prep race, and Hawthorne management obliged with a betless exhibition conducted between races on October 4, in which Round Table romped by seven.

For the Gold Cup — his nineteenth start of the year to date and sixteenth on the dirt — Bill Harmatz rode Round Table because Shoemaker was unavailable. The Jockey Club Gold Cup (at Belmont Park) was the same day and Shoemaker, perhaps beholden to Gallant Man's loyal and forgiving owner Ralph Lowe, a longtime friend and fellow Texan, opted to ride the Derby runner-up in the Belmont Park fixture. Gallant Man prevailed by a length in the two-mile Jockey Club Gold Cup.

The mile and a quarter Hawthorne Gold Cup proved a piece of cake for Round Table, though he faced the older Swoon's Son, considered the Midwest's top handicap horse. Swoon's Son was asked to concede seven pounds (128-121) to his younger foe. Round Table was the lone three-year-old in the line-up of six, which included the familiar form of Find.

Shortly after the start, Swoon's Son crossed in front of Round Table, after which Harmatz kept his colt just outside of the second favorite. Swoon's Son led

through a quarter in :22 1/5, a half-mile in :46 1/5, six furlongs in 1:10 3/5, and the mile in 1:35 1/5, all the while being stalked by Round Table.

With a furlong to go in the long Hawthorne stretch, Harmatz let Round Table roll, and he drew away from Swoon's Son with ease, reaching the wire three lengths to the good. Find once again was third, another two and a half lengths in arrears.

The final time of 2:00 1/5 was a Hawthorne record. The victory was the tenth in a row for Round Table.

The Hawthorne Gold Cup was Round Table's nineteenth appearance under colors in a campaign that began January 19. But he wasn't done yet — although perhaps he should have been.

The Trenton Handicap, a mile and a quarter race for three-year-olds and up scheduled for November 9 at Garden State Park, followed Belmont's Woodward on the Eastern fall racing schedule.

Eight days before the Trenton, at Molter's request, Round Table went through another of his betless exhibition prep races. He faced two rivals and won by eight lengths. The Round Table camp must have been encouraged that the mile and seventy-yard race was run over a "sloppy" strip. Round Table got hold of it well and just galloped.

This may have led to an unjustified confidence when the track came up "good" on the day of the Trenton, with the 1957 Horse of the Year honors on the line. Scratches reduced the field to three — the big three of Gallant Man (weighted at 124), Round Table (also 124), and Bold Ruler (122).

Actually, the Trenton Handicap was one of two options available to Round Table, Gallant Man, and Dedicate, for all three had been invited to participate in the Washington, D.C., International at a mile and one-half on the grass on November 11. However, all three declined, their connections expressing a preference for the Trenton.

The Trenton lacked the cachet of several other autumn stakes races, but its purse of $75,000 was a solid lure. Dedicate's people, however, opted to freshen him after he had been assigned high weight of 128 pounds by Ty Shea, the Garden State racing secretary. Dedicate's defection reduced the Trenton field to three — the three best three-year-olds in training.

This race set up as hugely advantageous for Bold

Ruler. If he were to be beaten, Bold Ruler had to be pressed early, as he was in the Belmont Stakes when Gallant Man's trainer John Nerud employed a "rabbit" to good effect. But in the Trenton, under a heady ride by Eddie Arcaro, Bold Ruler went about his business unpressured, and the Wheatley Stable runner cruised to a two and a quarter-length win over Gallant Man in 2:01 3/5, wrapping up his Horse of the Year title in the *Daily Racing Form* poll. (Dedicate was voted Horse of the Year by the Thoroughbred Racing Associations. It would be another fourteen years before the two organizations combined forces to produce the annual Eclipse Awards that determine the year's champions.)

Round Table was never in the race and straggled in eight and a half lengths behind Gallant Man. "Running off his hocks," as usual, he also ran down behind badly (scraped his heels) on the off-track. Such a wet surface was definitely not conducive to his running style. If the track was not hard and dry, Round Table was in trouble, for he had a reaching stride that demanded "purchase" if he were to do his best. He did not get it at Garden State Park that day.

The victory was the fourth in a row for Bold Ruler,

his eleventh of the season, and it secured the championship honors for the son of Nasrullah over his two rivals that day.

While Molter was recognized for doing an outstanding job in keeping Round Table going through such an extended campaign, the thought among many was that he, or Kerr, had "gone to the well one time too often" when they penciled in the Trenton.

Or, as Molter suggested in a *Daily Racing Form* interview the following year, perhaps they had gone to the wrong well. "Round Table should have run in the Washington, D.C., International (on grass)," Molter said, "but circumstances dictated otherwise.

"I still think Round Table could handle mud," Molter insisted, "but he couldn't handle mud and Bold Ruler."

Had Round Table opted for the International instead, or had Kerr merely passed the Trenton and let his little colt rest on his already considerable laurels, Round Table probably would have been voted the three-year-old championship as well as the Horse of the Year title, both of which went to Bold Ruler.

Instead, he would conclude his amazingly ambitious

campaign of twenty-two starts with a record of fifteen wins, one second, three thirds, and earnings of $600,383 — the most of any horse that year.

Despite making only three starts on the grass, Round Table was voted the first of what would be three consecutive turf titles.

ROUND TABLE

CHAPTER 6

Surpassing

After a seven-week respite from competition following the Trenton Handicap loss, Round Table in effect launched his memorable four-year-old campaign three days before the 1958 season began.

Under 130 pounds, Round Table won Santa Anita's seven-furlong Malibu Stakes on December 28, 1957. He gained his victory by a head in a bitter stretch battle with the hard-hitting Irish-bred Seaneen, to whom he was conceding sixteen pounds. The winning time was an excellent 1:22. As it turned out, the colt who couldn't win at Santa Anita the previous year couldn't lose there in 1958.

Round Table went off at fifteen cents to the dollar in the Malibu, marking the beginning of an extraordinary stretch of public confidence in an American racehorse. Round Table would continue as the favorite in thirty-one straight races — through the Manhattan Handicap in October of 1959. He would win twenty-four of those races, going unplaced only three times.

Travis Kerr had two primary goals for Round Table in 1958. Kerr wanted his $175,000 colt to exceed the million-dollar mark in career earnings, and he wanted him to replace Nashua as the world's leading money winner.

Kerr would be satisfied on both these counts, and many others as well, for Round Table in 1958 would not only shatter the existing monetary standards but rack up these accomplishments as well:

• Beginning with the Malibu, he would put together another impressive winning streak, this one measuring eight.

• In a three-month span, February 15 to May 11, he would set four track records and equal another without ever being really extended.

• Equal a world record.

• Win his first seven races of the season by a combined total of thirty-one and a half lengths.

• Win fourteen of his twenty starts in an arduous campaign stretching from the start of the year into the second week of October.

• By winning his first seven races of 1958 boost his record to an amazing nineteen wins in his last twenty starts in a year's span. (As *The Blood-Horse* noted, he was approaching "wonder horse status.")

• Compete at nine tracks in five states (California, Florida, Illinois, New Jersey, and New York) and Mexico.

• Carry 130 pounds or more a dozen times, winning seven, including three record runs. When he lost under these burdens it was usually either because he was being asked to concede chunks of weight or because he encountered "off" tracks.

• Win more than $600,000 for the second straight season, becoming the first horse in history to do so.

• Set a new world earnings record of $1,336,489.

• Gain Horse of the Year honors and be voted champion handicap horse while also repeating as champion turf horse.

It took a terrifically hardy specimen to thrive on such a regimen, but that was Round Table. In his maturity, Round Table stood 15.3 hands and weighed approximately 1,050 pounds. Horsemen assessing him invariably stressed his balance and correctness as his

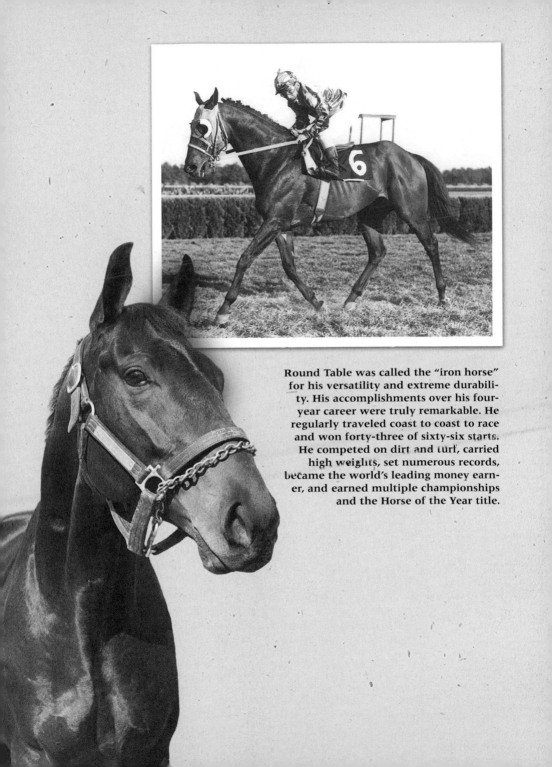

Round Table was called the "iron horse" for his versatility and extreme durability. His accomplishments over his four-year career were truly remarkable. He regularly traveled coast to coast to race and won forty-three of sixty-six starts. He competed on dirt and turf, carried high weights, set numerous records, became the world's leading money earner, and earned multiple championships and the Horse of the Year title.

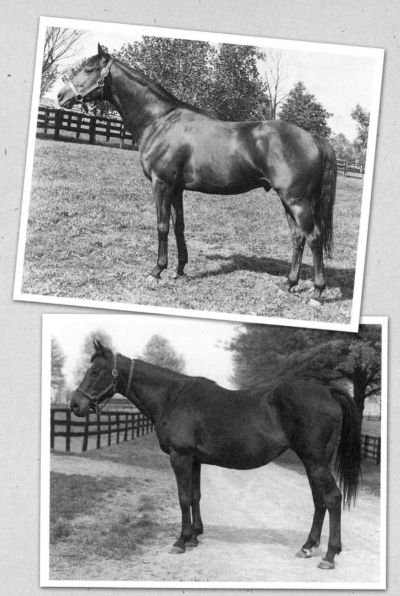

Round Table was the product of imported bloodlines. His sire, Princequillo (top), was bred in France, foaled in England, shipped to Ireland with his dam, Cosquilla, then sent to America to escape the encroaching World War II. He later was acquired by Claiborne Farm master Arthur Hancock Sr. Hancock's son, Bull Hancock, purchased Round Table's dam, Knight's Daughter (above), during a visit to England's Royal Stud. Her "sprinting blood" proved to be a perfect match with Princequillo's stamina influence.

Breeder Bull Hancock (right) sold Round Table to "save the farm" after his father died. New owner, Oklahoma oilman Travis Kerr (below, far right with Round Table, trainer Bill Molter, on far left, wife Jerry Kerr, and groom Juan Alaniz), was a hands-on owner who hotwalked Round Table on occasion. The Kerrs and Molter visited many winner's circles with their star (above).

Moody Jolley (left) trained Round Table for Claiborne Farm. After being purchased by Kerr, Round Table joined Bill Molter's stable. Molter (below on pony, leading Round Table to the track) had saddled Determine to win the 1954 Kentucky Derby before taking on Round Table in 1957.

"Strongman" Steve Brooks (top aboard
Round Table at two) was the colt's first
regular rider, and Ralph Neves (right)
rode Round Table five consecutive times
at three. But Bill Shoemaker (above)
paired with the hardy little horse the
most — thirty-three times or half of
Round Table's sixty-six starts.

Carrying Claiborne Farm's colors at two, Round Table won the Lafayette Stakes (above) at Keeneland's spring meet for his first stakes win, then returned in the fall to take the Breeders' Futurity (below).

"Keeneland's Lad" (left) returned to the Lexington track in the spring of 1957 to win the Blue Grass Stakes (below) en route to the Kentucky Derby. In one of the greatest fields ever assembled, Iron Liege (above, on lead in final turn) held off Gallant Man and Shoemaker (No. 5, fifth back), who misjudged the finish line. Round Table (No. 4 on inside) and Bold Ruler (No. 7 on outside) finished third and fourth, respectively.

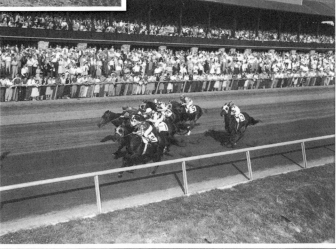

Sent to California after the Derby, Round Table finished second to older horses in the Californian before going on a five-race win streak in the Golden State. Among his victories were the Will Rogers Stakes (left) and the Westerner Handicap (above). He continued to win in Chicago, where he first ran on turf. His four-length romp in the American Derby (below) at Washington Park was clear evidence of his turf prowess, and his three victories in 1957 on that surface earned him his first grass championship.

Round Table began his four-year-old season a bit early, winning the Malibu Stakes (below right) in late December of 1957. The victory propelled him on an eight-race win streak that included the San Fernando Stakes (below left) and San Antonio and Santa Anita handicaps. After another second in the Californian, Round Table added victories in the Argonaut (left) and Arch Ward Memorial on the grass (above).

Round Table's competitive nature more than made up for his small stature. He rarely lost a photo, as shown by his narrow victory in the 1958 Laurance Armour (below). But many of his wins were by daylight like the 1958 Hawthorne Gold Cup (left). While at the track, Round Table was cared for by Juan Alaniz (bottom), who later would groom another great horse, Affirmed.

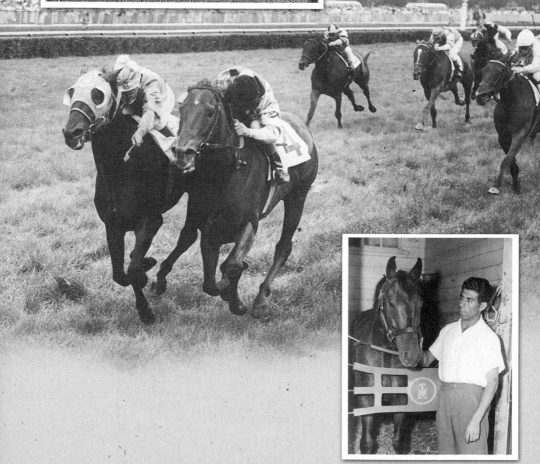

In January 1959 Round Table easily won the San Marcos (bottom) on the grass, but a subsequent injury kept him out of action until June. Upon his return, it was business as usual with a victory in the Citation Handicap (right). He later added a triumph in the Arlington Handicap (below).

Round Table (left, working out) thrived on his busy schedule, but even his racing days had to come to an end. His final two victories appropriately enough showcased his amazing versatility. He won the United Nations Handicap (top) on the grass carrying 136 pounds, then the Manhattan Handicap (above) on the dirt under 132 pounds.

Travis Kerr and Bill Molter bid their champion goodbye
and sent him to Claiborne Farm in Kentucky (below,
arriving in November 1959) where the unflashy but big-
hearted horse would stand at stud.

Round Table was a superb stallion, siring eighty-three stakes winners, including the filly Drumtop (right), King Pellinore (above), and Royal Glint (below).

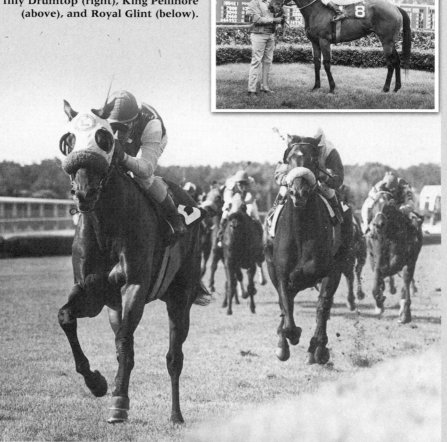

Leading sire of 1972, Round Table also was represented by English and Irish champion Apalachee (above right), crack sprinter King's Bishop (above left), and Canadian Horse of the Year He's a Smoothie (below).

Round Table reigned at Claiborne Farm from 1960 until his death in June of 1987. Three years before his death, Round Table received a visit from royalty when Queen Elizabeth II made a special effort to see him during her tour of Central Kentucky. It was a tribute befitting the grand old warrior.

ROUND TABLE
1954 — 1987

major physical attributes. There was nothing flashy about him. Round Table was not a "picture horse," until you discerned his nearly perfect symmetry, and until he started running. Then this amazingly healthy, durable, competitive, and versatile runner shone like polished silver.

As *Daily Racing Form*'s Charles Hatton noted, "The anatomy of Round Table equipped him well for the long, rough road down which his monetary Muse led him. He will serve nicely to illustrate that the most valuable things often come in small packages.

"Kerr and Company's champion," Hatton went on, "is a charming individual and perhaps the smallest specimen of his transcendent class to have graced the racing stage in many seasons. A David, if you please. One with the corky and audacious demeanor to suggest that his diminutive frame contains a great heart.

"Round Table is a scant 15.3 hands at the withers. There are many larger thoroughbreds who have yet to come of racing age. But rivals a hand taller have found the Kerr colt an opponent of unremitting courage in stretch duels."

Round Table made his first start of 1958 on January 11 in the San Fernando Stakes. He had an easy time in this mile and one-sixteenth test, reporting home four and a quarter lengths the best in 1:42 1/5. Runner-up The Searcher was in receipt of sixteen pounds (130 to 114).

Next up was the $156,990 Santa Anita Maturity two weeks later. With Shoemaker sitting out a suspension, Bill Harmatz once again deputized.

Shoemaker was a convivial and responsive companion in the jockeys' room, but otherwise in those days was as economical with words as a captured spy. When he was asked earlier that week whether he thought "anything can beat Round Table in the Maturity," Shoe replied, "Nope."

Some intrepid reporters continued the interrogation.

"Do you think anything can beat him if it comes up mud?"

"Nope," replied the man known then as the "Taciturn Texan."

"Not even (the good off-track performer) Promised Land?"

"Nope."

Shoemaker then smiled and took pity on his persis-

tent questioners, stringing entire sentences together. "Promised Land gets only a pound from Round Table," he pointed out. "It'll take a bigger weight spread than that to bring those two horses together."

Shoemaker knew whereof he spoke. After being bumped leaving the gate, Round Table quickly recovered and went to the lead. There he remained, arriving four and a half lengths in front of Seaneen, with Promised Land another three parts of a length back in third. Round Table went off at 1-10. Under the allowance conditions, he carried 126 pounds while covering the ten furlongs in 2:01 4/5.

In this race, as in many others, Round Table was eased at the end. The idea, of course, was to keep the margin of victory as modest as possible, especially when the handicapper would assign weights for a subsequent start.

Santa Anita racing secretary and handicapper James E. "Jimmy" Kilroe tacked on four pounds for Round Table's next start, the February 15 San Antonio Handicap at a mile and one-eighth. Shoemaker was back in the saddle as the Kerr runner took on a field of eight.

Despite the added weight, bettors made Round Table the .45-l choice. He responded with the first of his *five consecutive record* performances.

At the break Shoemaker took a strong hold on Round Table. They saved ground into the first turn and were fourth after the first half-mile as Seaneen showed the way. Entering the backstretch, Round Table was pinned on the rail. But at the five-furlong marker Find bore out slightly, and Round Table slithered through the small opening and into the lead without any urging and without brushing a rival. It was an impressive display of broken field running by this agile and very willing competitor.

Once Round Table was in the clear on the outside, the race was over. Shoemaker tapped him lightly entering the stretch and the colt drew out to tally by three and a half lengths. The final time of 1:46 4/5 equaled the world record, an announcement greeted by sustained applause from Round Table's numerous Santa Anita backers.

Reviewing Round Table's San Antonio performance a day later, *Daily Racing Form* columnist Oscar Otis took to the film room with Santa Anita patrol judge and film analyst Alfred Shelhamer. The two men watched several of Round Table's races in slow motion, concluding with the San Antonio. Otis had these observations to offer:

"Round Table's action is entirely different in style from horses like (other West Coast stars) Swaps or Noor. These horses, when at their best, seemed to glide...Round Table is just the opposite, for while he doesn't actually get high in the air either, he really works and puts his will to action in a manner that is readily discernible.

"With Swaps, Noor, or even going back to Citation, it was almost impossible to detect them changing leads. Not so with Round Table. In the San Antonio, when he changed going into the far turn and again entering the stretch, the switch was so sharp that he appeared to lift Shoemaker out of the saddle," Otis wrote.

On a couple of occasions during that Santa Anita meeting in the winter of 1958, rumors had it that Round Table had taken some "gimpy steps" with his left hind leg, suggesting he was hurting.

Peters, who had served as Round Table's veterinarian since facilitating his purchase, responded that his prime client "never takes a gimpy step. But it is true that on at least one occasion, when nearing the gate before a race, he has stepped short with his left hind. He did this in Florida before the sale and I almost turned him down because of it.

"However," said Peters, "the more I studied this horse the more I became convinced that this was just a nervous trait, nothing more. It is just possible that at one time in his life he had a tinge of stifle trouble. There is probably no such thing as a perfectly sound racehorse — I've never known a good horse that was absolutely flawless. But Round Table is the soundest horse I have ever known.

"This trait (with his left hind) is meaningless because he races sound. What's more, I have never known a horse whose races seemingly take less out of him. He came out of his (record-breaking) San Antonio kicking and playing as if the race had been nothing more than a good gallop," Peters said.

Stretching out to a mile and a quarter in the March 1 Santa Anita Handicap, and toting 130 pounds, proved to be no more difficult for Round Table than the San Antonio. He bested Terrang (119 pounds) by two and a

half lengths and set a Santa Anita record of 1:59 4/5. (Noor had established the previous mark eight years earlier while carrying only 110.) That Round Table went off at fifteen cents to the dollar in one of the country's major handicap events was testimony as to the regard in which Californians held him. Second choice in the wagering that day was third-place finisher Porterhouse, a 14-1 shot.

With handicapper Kilroe prepared to heft an additional four pounds aboard their colt for the mile and three-quarters San Juan Capistrano over the Santa Anita grass course, the Kerr camp politely declined and bought airline tickets for Florida. They had no compunction about trying South Florida with this seasoned tourist of theirs.

As Peters put it, "Round Table's a good little shipper, and if the flying weather should get a little rough, he'll eat more instead of less. During takeoffs he looks out a window, apparently liking to see the lights slide past. After the plane is up, he'll turn to the hay rack right away."

Engaging in his usual prep, Round Table for the first time faced the good Chilean-bred handicap horse

Meeting, recent winner of the rich Hialeah Turf Cup. At the end of the mile and one-sixteenth allowance race on March 14, Round Table cracked the track mark when he sped home in 1:41 3/5, three and a half lengths in front of Meeting.

The Gulfstream Park Handicap eight days later resulted in a virtual rerun. Shortly after the start, Meeting, under jockey John Ruane, crossed over abruptly, forcing Shoemaker to steady Round Table. But Round Table, giving Meeting nineteen pounds (130 to 111), proceeded to trounce his rival by four lengths in record time: 1:59 4/5 for the mile and a quarter, matching Coaltown's nine-year-old standard. Meeting had set the pace to the top of the stretch with Round Table stalking him, but they parted company when Shoemaker delivered one left-handed swat with his stick. Once again, Round Table won "with speed in reserve."

Bold Ruler and Gallant Man had yet to appear under colors in 1958, and with Round Table so dominant, it was suggested the Kerr colt be sent on a barnstorming tour of the nation's tracks to run against time, not live opponents, as the legendary trotter Dan Patch

had done years previous. Kerr never gave serious thought to this proposition.

With his charge having already made six starts since the first of the year, Molter had Round Table flown back to Hollywood Park with a lengthy freshening in mind for him. However, Caliente president John Alessio decided to revive the dormant Caliente Handicap on May 11 under conditions that prompted veteran racing official Francis Dunn to term the event the "Travesty Handicap." Kerr decided to return Round Table to action a bit earlier than planned in this $51,950 race.

Caliente officials assigned Round Table a mere 126 pounds against an undistinguished field, and he rolled to a nine and a quarter-length win in record time of 1:41 1/5 for a mile and one-sixteenth while performing at odds of 1-10. It was Round Table's fifth straight record effort.

Actually, the race produced some worrisome moments for the chalk players. Perhaps not as sharp as usual after his six-week hiatus, Round Table was outrun to the first turn and was caught in a speed jam, forcing Shoemaker to take up sharply and guide Round

Table off the rail. Once clear, Shoemaker brought Round Table four wide entering the stretch and had to rally him sharply before he pulled away. Though the strip was labeled "good," most observers deemed it just a shade off "fast." Nevertheless, Round Table reduced the Caliente record by a full second.

The win was worth $31,950, enough to push Round Table's career earnings to $1,005,760. He thus joined Nashua ($1,288,565) and Citation ($1,085,760) as horse racing's only millionaires. Round Table returned $2.20 to win and $2.20 to place. There was no show wagering, but the total pool of $94,846 was still a new one-race Caliente record. Of that total, some eighty-four percent ($79,450) cascaded through the mutuel windows on Round Table.

Even though the Caliente prize was seen as a "gift" by many in racing, the Kerrs were elated. Besides the historic purse, they received a specially designed solid silver sombrero trophy. And the fact remained, as noted by *Daily Racing Form*'s Leon Rasmussen, that the first $906,036 of Round Table's bankroll had been earned the hard way — "carrying top weight against the best available competition in

practically every section of the country, over both dirt and grass courses. No one has to make an excuse for this colt."

ROUND TABLE

CHAPTER 7

Title Triple

R ound Table, undefeated in seven starts as a four-year-old, had now won nineteen of his last twenty races. The Caliente 'Cap was his nineteenth stakes score in thirty-nine lifetime appearances.

Two weeks after Round Table returned from Mexico, he suffered a defeat that shocked the Turf world. Held at odds of fifteen cents to the dollar in the $108,000 Californian, he fell victim to old foe Seaneen, who beat him four and a quarter lengths while in receipt of twenty-one pounds (130 to 109).

That result soon took on the look of an aberration, for only two weeks after the upset Round Table made history in the one-mile Argonaut Handicap. Despite having lost the Californian, he was required to pick up an additional two pounds for this race. It did not prove an easy task. Coming from off the pace, Round Table gained a hard-fought nose victory over the speedy How Now while spotting him sixteen pounds. The time was 1:34 3/5, which ranked as the fastest mile in history under an impost of more than 130 pounds.

Travis Kerr credited Molter for returning Round Table in the Argonaut. "If I'd had my way to start with, Round Table wouldn't have started," Kerr said. "But after 'smoking' it over with Bill, he convinced me that it was the thing to do. I was rather upset prior to the race that the weight ceiling (130 pounds), which had applied to other horses here in recent years, was suddenly lifted. But Bill convinced me that Round Table was up to the challenge and that we could scuttle a lot of false rumors about being afraid of the (high) weights, etc. Nevertheless, I'm glad this race is in the record books."

In Molter's view, Round Table's Argonaut — in which he "gave lots of weight to good horses" — was his "best race since the (1957) United Nations. He went to his knees at the start of that one from his outside post-position, where the turf was deepest. He was on the outside of a spread on the first turn, he fought off challenge after challenge, and he had insect bites all over him, yet he still won under 130 pounds."

The Kerr camp now was faced with the depressing prospect of ever-increasing weight packages on the West Coast. With a series of rich stakes scheduled in Chicago, Round Table's connections decided to head there for the summer.

The nation's reigning grass champ made his first start of 1958 over that surface at Washington Park on June 20. It came in one of the preps Molter often sought leading up to his first big objective for Round Table, which in this case was the Arch Ward Handicap. With Ismael Valenzuela subbing for Shoemaker, Round Table took the betless exhibition by two lengths from Bernburgoo. He came back eight days later, equipped with Shoe, and polished off the Arch Ward by two and a half lengths, missing the track record for the mile and three-sixteenths by one-fifth of a second while well in hand. Tall Chief II, another Molter trainee, was second. Bernburgoo was fifth, beaten some seven lengths, one position in front of Mahan, who had been runner-up to Round Table in the 1957 grass champion balloting.

The victory in the Ward was Round Table's thirtieth in forty-three career starts. The winner's share of $33,000 pushed his earnings to $1,090,014. He, there-

fore, moved past Citation into second place.

Molter once said of Round Table, "He always tries so hard, and he hits the ground so hard, that I wonder sometimes how sore he must be — how it must hurt him. But he never shows any evidence of soreness, even though his way of going must be causing him some discomfort, if not pain, especially on the main track."

It may, then, have been the nature of Round Table's action that made him comparatively more effective on grass. He seemed to skim the turf.

The great grass course jockey Johnny Adams once was asked whether he thought a horse's ability to run on the grass was an "inherited characteristic," as is generally accepted when it comes to superior mudders.

Responded Adams: "I don't believe inheritance is the same factor in grass ability as it is in ability to run in the mud. In my opinion, agility and action are the factors that distinguish a good grass horse. The turf is not nearly as smooth and level as the main track, and an agile horse, who can handle the uneven surface, and who can negotiate the sharper turns on grass courses has an edge."

Round Table had won the exhibition carrying a

mere 122, the Ward under 129, both over the Washington Park grass course. Returned to the 130-pound level and to the main track at Arlington Park for the $85,000 Warren Wright Memorial Handicap on July 12, he lost a heartbreaker to new rival Bernburgoo. The son of Bernborough was owned and trained by the "Midwest Claiming King," William Hal Bishop, a former mule trader from Anna, Illinois, who loved to refer to himself as "Old Nickels and Dimes."

A field of eight went to the post for the nine-furlong Wright. In the absence of Shoemaker, who was serving a suspension for careless riding, Johnny Longden rode Round Table, who was sent off at 3-10. Round Table carried his "usual" 130 pounds.

Longden, who hadn't ridden Round Table since losing the San Bernardino on him in March of the previous year, took his colt right to the lead in the Wright. With a furlong to go, Round Table opened up a two-length advantage. But he tired in the final furlong, and Bernburgoo (under 109 pounds) came along to post a stunning head victory. Bernburgoo was timed in a near-record 1:48 3/5 over the fast main track. It ranked as one of the major upsets in the history of Chicago racing.

Arlington Park vice president Bill Thayer recalled in 2001 that jockey "Clarence Meaux rode Bernburgoo, who went off at 20-1. He trailed the field early, started to make up ground, and Meaux brought him down the middle of the track and just nailed Round Table at the wire. Maybe Round Table didn't see him coming, because he usually beat horses he could see no matter what the weights were.

"Marje (Arlington president Marje Everett) had the Wright Handicap trophy all made up and ready to be presented," Thayer continued. "The problem was that the floral wreath that was supposed to surround it were in Travis Kerr's colors — yellow and green. Everybody, including Marje, had expected Round Table to win.

"Bishop got the trophy and the wreath. Was he insulted by the wreath that wasn't in his colors? No way. That was the biggest race Hal Bishop ever won. He didn't care about the flowers. He was concentrating on the ($53,900) winner's share."

(Bishop, who owned and trained 3,150 winners, once said, "I never wanted to win stakes races — just three races every day.")

A week after losing the Wright to Bernburgoo,

Molter returned Round Table to the turf for the $87,000 Laurance Armour Handicap at Arlington. In what would be an abbreviated pact, Kerr had engaged Bill Hartack to "handle Round Table for the rest of the season." Kerr was looking ahead to an anticipated meeting between Round Table and Gallant Man (it would never occur) and felt that Shoemaker's loyalty to Ralph Lowe would prompt him to ride Gallant Man.

One of the best grass stakes line-ups of the year was assembled for the Armour, including not only Round Table and Clem but also Mahan, previous year's winner of the prestigious Washington, D.C., International, and Tudor Era, who would finish first in that race later in 1958, only to be disqualified.

The Kerr-Hartack pact turned out to be a one-race deal, and not because of Hartack's performance, for he put up a tremendous finish on Round Table to win the Armour. After being boxed in all the way in the run down the backstretch, the 7-10 Round Table, under 130 pounds, shot through an opening on the turn and then charged down the outside to run down Clem (110) by a nose, equaling the track record of 1:48 2/5 for a mile and one-eighth. Said Hartack of Round

Table, "What a pro! He just wouldn't let that horse (Clem) beat him."

This was the first in a series of memorable confrontations between Round Table and Clem, owned by Mrs. Adele Rand, named for the famed sportscaster Clem McCarthy, and ridden by Ted Atkinson.

Describing the Armour in his *Daily Racing Form* column of July 22, Joe Hirsch termed it "one of the great races, the kind you'll remember for a long time, like Native Dancer's Metropolitan or Princess Turia's Kentucky Oaks or Nashua's Arlington Classic. Bill Molter concurred. 'His (1957) United Nations was unforgettable, but this one was exceptional.'

"When Ted Atkinson turned Clem loose at the head of the stretch, and Bill Hartack was finally able to secure racing room for Round Table, Chicago fans were treated to one of the most dramatic final furlongs seen in the Midwest in many a year. Relentlessly, Round Table narrowed the gap between these two courageous horses, but it took the judges interminable minutes before they were able to separate them in the closest of photos. On a million dollar horse, Hartack put up a million dollar ride," Hirsch wrote.

Clem's trainer, W.W. "Bill" Stephens, was left shaking his head, for this decision made for two straight heartbreaking defeats. "Two noses in the space of two weeks — Bold Ruler in the Suburban, and now Round Table," he lamented.

"I wouldn't want to choose between Bold Ruler and Round Table," Stephens added, "and I'd hate to run against the two of them together." (That possibility never arose, for Bold Ruler broke down under 136 pounds in the July 26 Brooklyn Handicap at Jamaica and was retired.)

Shoemaker was reinstated for Round Table's next start, a fifth-place finish in the $133,000 Equipoise Mile at Arlington Park on August 9. The one-mile test over the main track was won by Swoon's Son in a brisk 1:34 4/5. Round Table gave Swoon's Son two pounds (131 to 129) and never threatened. This was the first time Round Table had finished out of the money since March of 1957. But Shoe would be his rider in fifteen of the twenty-one subsequent races comprising Round Table's career.

Another grass win/dirt loss sequence followed. On August 23 Round Table carried 130 pounds to a two and a quarter-length triumph over Clem (109 pounds) in the $85,000 Arlington Handicap. His time of 1:54 2/5 was one tick off the track record for the mile and three-sixteenths and it was apparent Round Table could have easily set a new standard had Shoemaker asked for his best.

Clem got revenge when, on September 1, Round Table returned to the main track in the $139,000 Washington Park Handicap at one mile. And Clem had to break a twenty-six-year-old track record to do so.

Under 110 pounds, Clem sped the distance in 1:34. Round Table, toting 131, made up some ground late but still finished a well-beaten second, three and a quarter lengths back. Only a nose back in third came the good three-year-old Nadir, who was getting seventeen pounds from Round Table. Perhaps the bettors cottoned to Round Table's recent win-on-the-grass, lose-on-the-dirt pattern, for they sent him off at the relatively liberal odds of 2-1, the first time in ten months and fifteen races he'd been higher than odds-on.

Seven days after losing to Clem for the first time, Round Table prepped for the United Nations Handicap with a mile and one-sixteenth allowance race win.

Shoemaker was aboard for that tally but missed Round Table's next two starts, both of which were losses.

Attempting a repeat score in the September 13 United Nations under Ismael Valenzuela, Round Table failed by a half-length to catch Clem ("one tough customer," as Molter put it), who beat him for the second straight time in track-record time.

Getting seventeen pounds from Round Table, Clem led throughout with Round Table in close pursuit all the way around. Clem's time of 1:54 3/5 lowered the Atlantic City record by more than a second.

This was a significant event not only because of Clem's record run, for it marked the first time Round Table had been beaten on grass. He had rung up eight wins in a row before bowing to his nemesis.

Clem added insult to injury two weeks later at Belmont Park. Carrying 126 pounds under the weight-for-age conditions of the Woodward Stakes, Clem beat Nadir by a half-length as Round Table trailed in fifth, seventeen and a half lengths back in the worst finish of his career up to that point. Eddie Arcaro rode Round Table, the odds-on choice after the defection of Gallant Man, despite the sloppy condition of the track and

Round Table's well-known aversion to such going. Round Table showed speed for the first half-mile, then retreated. He came back to be unsaddled with both rear heels bleeding from his having run down badly.

Sports Illustrated's account of the Woodward said that before the race, in the paddock, Molter and Peters "made an important decision. On the theory that Round Table's rear run-down bandages might collect extra weight in the form of flying slop, the bandages were removed, and with them went Round Table's chances, for after running three-quarters of a mile with Clem, Belmont's gritty sand took its painful toll on Round Table's heels and he gave up...If this didn't earn him a long rest after facing the starter 41 times in the last two years, then it would be most unfair to a courageous colt."

Actually, following the Woodward, Kerr announced Round Table was retired for the season. However, only a few days later out came the weights for the Hawthorne Gold Cup, and Round Table was "unretired" and put on a plane for Chicago. With the money-won record so close at hand, the prospect of picking up a "mere" 126 pounds in the $123,850 race at

Hawthorne on October 11 beckoned powerfully.

According to Kerr, the decision was made "only after the recommendation of our vet, Dr. John Peters. Earlier, we had planned to end Round Table's campaign with the Woodward. But there were certain aspects of the Hawthorne Gold Cup, the main one being that he fancied that racetrack so much and ran brilliantly over it, that we felt we had enough margin of safety with the horse to chance this one race."

So, the intrepid traveler had his ticket punched one more time for the 1958 season. According to *Turf and Sport* writer Ellen Parker, Round Table's groom, Juan Alaniz (who years later would rub Triple Crown winner Affirmed), was asked by Molter before the Hawthorne race whether the colt was ready. "I told him that I could hardly hold him, he was so ready."

"Round Table made a believer out of me that fall," said Phil Georgeff, the longtime Chicago track announcer who retired in 1992. "I had seen Round Table as a two-year-old, and he wasn't that impressive. At three he was a heckuva lot better horse. But my big favorite in those years was Swoon's Son, who raced often and well in Chicago.

"When Round Table beat Swoon's Son in the 1957 Hawthorne Gold Cup and set a track record," Georgeff said, "I should have been won over. But I was stubborn. Swoon's Son had given Round Table seven pounds (128 to 121) that day and lost by three lengths. I remember that Bull Hancock said once that he thought Swoon's Son was the best horse in America.

"It was the 1958 Gold Cup that 'forced' me to admit that Round Table really was a great horse. Coming off that terrible race in the Woodward two weeks earlier, he was very impressive. Shoemaker sent Round Table right to the lead but he was headed by Swoon's Son after the first quarter. Swoon's Son (123 pounds) took over the lead for the rest of the first mile, with Round Table under a hold just outside him. When Shoe asked him, Round Table opened up easily on Swoon's Son and won going away. He made a convert out of me that afternoon."

Running the mile and a quarter in under two minutes for the fourth time, the seemingly indestructible Round Table lowered his own Hawthorne mark to 1:59 4/5. The winner's share of $74,850 elevated Round Table's earnings to $1,336,489 — a new world record.

Round Table also became the first horse to lead in purses won for two seasons.

Round Table had made many "converts" in addition to Georgeff in a season that saw him win fourteen of twenty starts at nine different tracks, eleven of those victories coming in stakes; set five track records, equal another two, and match a world mark while taking down $662,780; and carry an average weight of almost 129 pounds.

As Charles Hatton wrote, "Only a very comfortable shipper, an adaptable and even-tempered individual, and one of extraordinary soundness could have withstood such rigorous campaigning. The prerequisite of 'class' is understood in this abridged catechism."

Round Table's exploits helped propel the twenty-seven-year-old Shoemaker to the top of the jockeys' earnings ($2,961,693) and victories (three hundred) lists. And with $1,116,544 Molter won the first of two consecutive monetary crowns (he totaled four in all).

In the weeks leading up to the balloting for year-end honors, the quiet but occasionally outspoken Kerr made no secret of his feelings. "I don't know if Round Table will get Horse of the Year, but in my opinion it is just as plain as the head of a goat that he should get it. What does a horse have to do to deserve it?"

Kerr said he was tremendously disappointed by the Woodward result. "I think we made a mistake by sending him to the front early when he had been coming from off the pace...And while he has won on them, Round Table is not partial to 'off tracks.'

"But tell me what recent Horses of the Year didn't have some failing? Nashua's temperament got the better of him at times and he didn't always run the race he was capable of. Swaps ran twice on the turf and didn't distinguish himself. Bold Ruler got the honor although he won only one race at what is supposed to be our classic distance, one and a quarter miles.

"I'm not knocking these horses," Kerr said. "They are great horses. But I believe that Round Table is certainly just as great. After all, aren't soundness and durability outstanding attributes in a horse of his quality?"

Yes, they are. And the voters agreed with Kerr. Round Table was named Horse of the Year as well as top handicap horse and, for the second straight year, grass champion. He, thus, became the first horse to win three titles in a single, magnificent season.

Five And Fighting

In a day when star performers are whisked off the racetrack and into syndicated stud duty after careers of a dozen or two races, it seems almost unimaginable that Round Table returned to competition at age five despite being a multiple champion and Horse of the Year who had already started fifty-two times en route to thirty-four victories.

But Travis Kerr had a point to make — that Round Table was a great horse. So the determined Oklahoman and his redoubtable little runner went about doing so in 1959.

It was not an easy task. Whereas in 1958 racing secretaries had pretty much established 130 pounds as top weight, in 1959 they raised the ceiling. Round Table was required to carry 132 pounds eight times, 134 pounds once, and 136 on another occasion.

Despite these burdens, and the demands of another coast-to-coast campaign, Round Table chalked up nine wins from his fourteen starts that season, eight of them in stakes. He also broke or equaled another six records to set the seal on a career that, for sustained brilliance, may never be witnessed again.

Molter selected Santa Anita's seven-furlong San Carlos Handicap on January 3 for Round Table's 1959 debut. The result was a loss on the racetrack, but not in stature, for this was one of Round Table's very best career efforts. Carrying 132 pounds, he was beaten a head by Hillsdale (115) in 1:21 4/5 after putting up a terrific fight. Entering the stretch, Hillsdale slipped through an opening on the rail while Bill Shoemaker had to swing Round Table to the outside to avoid traffic. This loss of ground, plus the weight differential, left Round Table with an impossible task.

Leon Rasmussen wrote in *Daily Racing Form* that "last Saturday's San Carlos…was one of the most thrilling and remarkable and unforgettable races ever witnessed by this observer. It takes rank with the memorable 'match' between Noor and Citation in the San Juan Capistrano of 1950 and the Tom Fool-Royal Vale struggle in the Suburban in 1958.

"After the race trainer Willie Molter said it so well: 'I have to keep smilin' to keep from cryin.'

"The 1958 Horse of the Year was every inch a champion even in defeat," Rasmussen concluded.

The contentious San Carlos proved to be an ideal prep for Round Table's appearance three weeks later in the mile and a quarter San Marcos Handicap. This was the first of seven turf races on Round Table's 1959 agenda, six of which he would win, and it stamped him solidly as the so-called "Man o' War of grass racing" after he produced a new American record.

Shoemaker shot Round Table right to the lead in the San Marcos, and there they stayed. Round Table was in front by two lengths after a half-mile in :45 3/5, maintained that margin through six furlongs in 1:09 4/5, then drew out by five lengths after a mile in a torrid 1:33 4/5 to win eased up.

Five lengths was Round Table's final margin over Eddie Schmidt, to whom he conceded sixteen pounds. The final time was 1:58 2/5. Not only was the new standard accomplished as Round Table toted 132 pounds, but it marked the fifth time in his career that he would traverse ten furlongs in less than two minutes — an unprecedented and subsequently unmatched achievement. Furthermore, he cracked two minutes while twice carrying 130 pounds, another time with 132 up. By the time he was retired, Round Table would have carried between 130 and 136 pounds twenty-five times, winning seventeen times. The mind boggles.

The Santa Anita fans cheered Round Table to the skies following what would be his final victory at the Arcadia oval. A jubilant Travis Kerr stated in the winner's circle, "This is the world's greatest horse."

But the Kerr-Round Table combine soon plummeted from this emotional pinnacle. First, racing secretary-handicapper Jimmy Kilroe assigned Round Table 135 pounds for the San Antonio Handicap on February 16. The Kerrs politely declined.

Then, for the February 23 Washington's Birthday Handicap at a mile and a half on the turf, Kilroe slightly relented and took a pound off. The Kerrs sent Round Table out under 134 pounds onto a soggy turf course. Round Table stumbled coming out of the gate, cutting off a small chunk of his front left hoof. Though he quickly recovered and moved into second place,

Round Table just as quickly evidenced signs of distress. Shoemaker noted them, ushered him around, and Round Table galloped in thirty lengths behind the victorious Hakuchikara. A 45-1 shot, Hakuchikara became the first Japanese-bred to win a stakes in the United States.

One press report said Shoemaker was "apparently unaware of the injury" and said only that Round Table "did not like" the sodden course. Shoemaker said in 2001 that he knew at the time something was "physically wrong" with his longtime partner. "When I brought him back to be unsaddled, I told the groom that the horse was in bad shape," Shoemaker recalled.

The wound bled for some thirty minutes after Round Table was returned to his stall. The next morning, Kerr announced that Round Table would be sidelined until the Hollywood Park summer meeting.

This injury was actually the second in slightly more than a week for Round Table. On February 15, eight days prior to the Washington's Birthday, after galloping over a sloppy Santa Anita strip that had been tightly sealed, Round Table came back with a slight quarter crack on his right front hoof.

Not all such injuries — cracks in the wall of the hoof running downward from the coronet — require removing a horse from training. Round Table's injury was only a half-inch long and back near the heel. This was the "iron horse's" first injury since he stepped on a nail as a two-year-old.

John Peters traced the injury to an incident in early December. Round Table had been rolling around happily in his sand pile near the Molter barn, "having a great time," the veterinarian said. "When he gets up, he is like a bucking bronco — he explodes, he is so full of life. That particular morning, when he 'exploded,' he grabbed himself, tearing a piece of flesh slightly bigger than a quarter out of the coronet band." Peters added he believed as the bruise grew down to the hoof it weakened the surrounding area, eventually producing the quarter crack.

Training up to the Washington's Birthday, Round Table was equipped with a steel bar shoe on his right hoof but wore a standard aluminum plate in the race.

The concurrence of these injuries, relatively slight but nevertheless aggravating, prompted Kerr to order a vacation for Round Table, who amazingly enough had *never* been out of training or off the racetrack since his career debut three years earlier.

In late March, Kerr reported that "Round Table's injuries are healing very nicely, and we believe there is less chance of aggravating this trouble running him on the turf. As this is Round Table's last campaign before going to stud, and inasmuch as he has now attained the sport's highest honor (Horse of the Year), we are not looking for new worlds for Round Table to conquer. He has proved himself a weight carrier and proficient over both the dirt and the grass. Weighing these factors, we decided to first concentrate on a grass course campaign in the Chicago area."

Round Table's incredible resiliency was evident when he came off the shelf firing on June 13, 1959, at Washington Park. Kerr had stuck with his announced plan to ship to the Midwest, but he and Molter chose a one-mile dirt race, the Citation Handicap, not a grass event, as the vehicle of Round Table's return to action. And what a return it was!

Despite not having raced in some fifteen weeks, Round Table picked up 130 pounds in the Citation and prevailed by a neck after a fierce stretch fight with

Etonian (who had a mere 104 pounds). Round Table, even after being bumped and nearly knocked off his feet, equaled Swaps' track record time of 1:33 2/5.

With Steve Brooks aboard for the second straight time, Round Table returned to the turf with an easy score in an exhibition race at Washington Park on June 25. Shoemaker was back on duty for Round Table's next start, the Stars and Stripes Handicap on July 4.

Relishing the firm turf course — arguably his favorite kind of going (he would wind up with thirteen wins in fourteen starts over it) — Round Table won with ease. His eight rivals included such top turf horses as Tudor Era, Manassas, and One-Eyed King. The latter brought a four-race win streak into the fray and left it there. Round Table sped the nine furlongs in 1:47 2/5, carving a second and two-fifths from the track record and setting a new American record in the process. Runner-up Noureddin, with his 110 pounds, was getting twenty-two from the victor. After dismounting, Brooks, who rode Anxious Moment, told newsmen that Round Table was the best horse he had ever been aboard.

Peters marveled at the recuperative powers of his

most famous patient. Round Table was the soundest and healthiest horse "ever to step onto a track," Peters said.

Round Table's well-being was briefly jeopardized one day that Chicago summer by the ill-advised actions of a young Molter stable employee named William Nack. A native of Skokie, Illinois, Nack later would become an Eclipse Award-winning Turf writer and author of the definitive book on Secretariat (*Big Red of Meadow Stable*). But that summer following his senior year in high school, Nack hotwalked horses for Molter.

As Nack recalled in a memoir published in *Sports Illustrated* in 1989, "The class of the barn was Round Table, who used to stand for hours with his head out of the stall, swaying side to side incessantly, like a fighter warming up. He was already on his way to the Hall of Fame as perhaps the greatest grass runner in history. (But) it was a wonder, with John (Nack's friend and co-worker John McGinnis) and me in the barn, that Round Table made it through the season.

"One afternoon," Nack continued, "we were sitting around the tack room behind Round Table's stall, and I had one of the most harebrained ideas of my

life...John and I were talking about jockeys and race riding, how they whoop and holler coming out of the gate. So I took a saddle, put it over the sawhorse and climbed aboard to demonstrate. I hitched up the stirrups, reached over and took some reins of a bridle in my hands. I told John to take that stirrup off the wall...and bang the inside of it with that screwdriver, so as to make the sound of a starting-gate bell. Hunching over, I said, 'Go!'

"McGinnis banged on the stirrup as if he were calling the whole racetrack to dinner. I started yelling and slapping the sides of the sawhorse. And all of a sudden, it was as if the barn had gone up in flames. There were horses screaming all over the shed, and I looked up and saw Round Table's forelegs reaching over the top of the stall. Terrified, I fell motionless. Mr. Hack (the stable foreman) bounded into the tack room. He was white. 'What in da hell are you boys doin'?' he cried. 'You wanna kill every horse in da barn?' "

Perhaps emboldened by Round Table's three straight triumphs in his comeback, his connections sent him out on a sloppy racing strip for the Equipoise Mile Handicap on August 8. It was the last time he would attempt such footing. As if emphasizing his dislike for the conditions, Round Table broke very poorly and was well back early, a scenario vastly different from that of his good races. He managed to get up for third behind Better Bee (115), to whom he was conceding seventeen pounds.

Back on the grass, Round Table, under 132 pounds, gave Tudor Era seventeen pounds and eked out a neck victory over him in an overnight handicap (the Clem McCarthy, no less) on grass at Arlington Park, August 15. His weight-carrying feats had begun to verge on the ho-hum.

Earlier that summer, *Daily Racing Form*'s Joe Hirsch said Round Table's ranking in unofficial racing fan polls puzzled him. "By the sheer weight of accomplishment," Hirsch wrote, Round Table "must be ranked with the great horses of modern times, and yet oddly enough he has never seemed to catch the fancy of the public like a Native Dancer or a Stymie."

Round Table strongly remedied that situation in his next three starts, the first two before his Chicago fans, the other a triumphant return to the Jersey Shore. These extraordinary efforts in the course of one month rank with any trio in the annals of American racing.

Again competing on Arlington's turf course, this time on August 22, Round Table again won a photo finish while at a huge weight disadvantage. It came in the $125,000, mile and three-sixteenths Arlington Handicap. Runner-up Manassas, beaten a head, carried just 112 pounds to Round Table's 132. Round Table's time of 1:53 2/5 was another American record — his third of the year.

Two weeks later, Round Table enjoyed one of the easiest wins of his life. With only mild encouragement from Shoemaker, he gave the good handicap horse Dunce eighteen pounds and a six and a half-length licking in the $122,000 Washington Park Handicap on September 7.

The Washington Park victory was significant from two standpoints. First, it resulted in Round Table's turning in his fifth record run of the season, as he matched the old course's nine-furlong standard of 1:47 1/5. Secondly, he had established his American record with exactly that same time in the Stars and Stripes two months earlier — also under 132 pounds, but on grass! He thus indelibly emphasized his brilliance, hardiness, and versatility in a display for the ages.

Round Table headed east, after his Washington Park 'Cap tour de force, to return to grass competition in the United Nations Handicap at Atlantic City on September 19. He had won this race by a nose as a three-year-old and lost by a half-length to Clem at four. This time, he was asked to heft the highest impost of his career — 136 pounds — in the mile and three-sixteenths event worth $100,000.

Naysayers in the Eastern racing press were dubious about Round Table's chances of succeeding. To one writer, Round Table's only East Coast successes had been two "hollow triumphs" at Gulfstream Park the previous year. Round Table's "record in the East has been infinitely less lustrous" than his ledger elsewhere, claimed this critic.

His critics were perhaps unaware that as a result of having been rested for a while, he probably was a much better and stronger specimen than he had been before incurring his quarter crack.

Of the whopping 136-pound package assigned Round Table for the United Nations, Travis Kerr commented: "We're realists. We know that 136 pounds is a lot of weight. But we're going to try it...Actually, we have come to feel that carrying 136 pounds with the next weighted horses also carrying respectable weights is more favorable than conceding some good horses 25 pounds, as he has been asked to do in the past.

"In the interest of racing and the horse," said the sportsman from Ada, Oklahoma, "we're going to pick up that weight."

Kerr also was looking beyond the United Nations. He said if Round Table emerged healthy from the Atlantic City test, he would be wheeled back *one week later* in the Woodward at Aqueduct.

Said Kerr: "I want to patronize the Woodward because it is a weight-for-age stakes and I feel this country is in dire need of more such races. This will not help me, because the law of averages is against my coming up with another Round Table, but I would like to see some other poor souls helped."

It is easy to understand Kerr's stance, for Round Table's was an era in which handicap races predominated for stakes horses. Round Table was required to make thirty-one starts while at the mercy of the handicapper. He almost always carried high weight in those races.

By the time of his 1959 fall campaign, Round Table

was beginning to receive his due on a national level. Writers continued to refer to him as the "Man o' War of the turf," pointing out that he had done things neither Swaps nor Citation ever did. The latter's trainer, Jimmy Jones, said Round Table was "the best grass horse I've ever seen."

Commented the *Racing Form*'s Hirsch: "We've been watching Round Table run for four years, and it is interesting to recall his status with each passing season. As a 2-year-old, they called him 'just another colt.' As a 3-year-old, despite a magnificent victory in the United Nations against older horses, they nodded knowingly at the results of the Trenton Handicap and called him the third best sophomore, behind Bold Ruler and Gallant Man. At 4, they grudgingly admired his durability and hesitantly voted him Horse of the Year, but complained about his lack of 'color.'

"Now, at 5, as he keeps winning the big ones with his weight up in the relentlessly professional thoroughness of the New York Yankees in Ruth's day and DiMaggio's, the applause grows louder with each passing hour until it is a crescendo of appreciation and admiration for one of the greatest performers in the history of U.S. racing."

The September 19 United Nations was perhaps Round Table's best race ever. Benefiting from a beautiful rating ride by Shoemaker, Round Table not only beat a top-notch field under his career-high burden but missed the Atlantic City track record by only three-fifths of a second. Round Table won by one and a quarter lengths over Noureddin. Tudor Era was back in fourth.

Ten horses contested the United Nations. As usual, Round Table was favored, 4-5 being his price on this occasion. Second choice at 3-1 was Noureddin, who had won a prep for the United Nations in impressive style. Third and fourth choices were Tudor Era and Li'l Fella, ridden, respectively, by men who had previously piloted Round Table: Bill Hartack and Bill Harmatz.

Li'l Fella shot to the early lead over the firm turf course, with Round Table in closest attendance and saving ground under Shoemaker. After Li'l Fella took the field through the first six furlongs, on top by two lengths, the Shoe let out a notch and guided Round Table to the outside nearing the final turn. Round Table quickly took command when asked in the upper stretch and, under intermittent urging, won "ridden out" by a length and a quarter.

Round Table's time under his whopping burden was an excellent 1:55 1/5. Clem had set the track mark of 1:54 3/5 in the same race the year before while carrying 113 pounds. Noureddin, who came on late to be a non-threatening second, packed nineteen pounds less than the winner. Li'l Fella and Tudor Era, who finished third and fourth, both carried 120.

Round Table ran a disappointing third as the 7-10 favorite behind three-year-old sensation Sword Dancer in the Woodward just one week later but bounced back with another memorable effort. Facing ten rivals in the mile and five-eighths Manhattan Handicap at Aqueduct on October 10, Round Table won by a length over the crack handicap horse Bald Eagle, conceding him ten pounds. Round Table's time of 2:42 3/5 was the sixteenth and final track-record performance of his career. It was also Round Table's seventh win of 1959 under 132 pounds or more.

Despite his record of nine wins in thirteen starts, it was believed that Round Table would have to avenge his Woodward defeat and beat Sword Dancer to gain a second Horse of the Year crown. So Kerr sent his wearied warrior out in the two-mile Jockey Club Gold Cup at the Big A on October 31. The plan failed, as Round Table trailed in seven lengths back of his younger rival.

Round Table's gleanings from this second-place finish in his final career start elevated his bankroll to $1,749,869. He was retired as the world's leading money winner. He had set or equaled one world record, three American records, and twelve track records. He was voted champion older horse of 1959 as well as his third consecutive grass championship.

Travis Kerr bade good-bye to Round Table "with mixed emotions. We hate to think we will never see him race again. Yet he has given us so much pleasure over the past three years that we want to be completely fair to him. I am pleased to say that he retires completely sound."

Said his saddened trainer in waving farewell to racing's greatest meal ticket to that point: "Round Table is as sound and willing a horse that ever has lived. Outside of a cut on one leg and slight quarter crack in his hoof last winter, he's been as perfect a specimen as you could find, anyplace or anytime.

"If you could design a horse like that for yourself," Bill Molter added, "well...you couldn't."

ROUND TABLE

EPILOGUE

Steady As A Clock

In 1960, as Round Table awaited the start of his stud career, *Daily Racing Form*'s Charles Hatton wrote: "Round Table's riders agree that he was steady as a clock, a cooperative racing 'tool' uncomplicated by any foibles. His manner in the paddock, on parade, and at the post is one of poise and composure. In the race itself he is an assured technician, not one to squander his resources in needless exuberance.

"Round Table makes an interesting prospective sire because he has these attributes," Hatton continued. "He should exert a strengthening influence on the breed. For all his lack of size, he is physically and intuitively a high-class racehorse. There are not many."

Round Table proved to be a major influence at stud, leading the sires money-won list in 1972 and turning out champions He's a Smoothie (Canada), Apalachee

126

(England), and Targowice (France) among eighty-three stakes winners, whose numbers also included million-aire Royal Glint and international stakes winner King Pellinore. Round Table is one of only eight North American sires in modern history to average twenty percent or more stakes winners from foals. The "magnificent eight" are as follows: Broomstick, twenty-five percent; Bold Ruler, Nasrullah and Northern Dancer, all twenty-three percent; Ultimus, twenty-two percent; Round Table and Hoist the Flag, both twenty-one percent; and Peter Pan, twenty percent. Round Table was a tremendously potent force as a sire of broodmares, also, as nearly fifty percent of his daughters that had foals produced stakes winners.

Author Abram S. Hewitt assessed Round Table this way: "He turned in a succession of wonderful performances; but we must not forget that he lost when he faced the best of his contemporaries, Gallant Man and Bold Ruler, and the younger Sword Dancer...He was no super horse, rather a first-class performer in one of the best foal crops in history."

Many disagreed with Hewitt. Among them were members of the panel of experts that in 1999 rated the top one hundred racehorses of the twentieth century for *The Blood-Horse*. They ranked Round Table seventeenth on the list, which was headed by Man o' War, with Bold Ruler nineteenth, Gallant Man thirty-sixth, and Sword Dancer fifty-third.

Also disagreeing with Hewitt was English racing journalist Tony Morris. In Morris' view, "great" was a designation to be earned "not from an impression of superiority derived from a total of 20 minutes racing, but from the proof of consistent merit displayed over a long period at the highest level of competition...No horse of the post-war era was better entitled to that description than Round Table," Morris wrote in 1983 in the *Racing Post*.

Perhaps he was not a super horse on dirt, but others believed Round Table qualified as that on the grass, a surface major foes like Bold Ruler and Gallant Man never attempted. Round Table's sixteen grass starts resulted in fourteen victories and four records. The only American grass campaigner talked about in the same breath as Round Table was the redoubtable John Henry, who won thirty of his fifty turf tests, four of them record runs.

John Henry carried as much as 130 pounds only twice in his eighty-three-race career. Round Table hefted those packages twenty-five times.

As racing writer Ellen Parker has noted, "In two important ways, Round Table was born before his time as a racehorse *and* as a sire. There were few turf courses and fewer big purses for turf stakes in the late 1950s. Considering his record on Arlington's turf course, imagine how successful he would have been in the Million alone! And considering his versatility, the Breeders' Cup Mile, Breeders' Cup Turf or the Breeders' Cup Classic would have been well within his capabilities."

In the spring of 1960, Bill Molter died of a heart attack in California. His "biggest horse," Round Table, had departed the stable by then, and Molter was launching the career of another star, T. V. Lark, at the time of his death. Later that year, Molter was posthumously inducted into the Racing Hall of Fame with a career record of 2,158 wins and purses totaling $11,938,035.

Round Table's first conditioner, Moody Jolley, passed away at age sixty-five in Hialeah Hospital on

February 4, 1976. *The Blood-Horse* reported at the time, "Some people thought that Moody Jolley's name fit the man perfectly. Art Grace, Florida correspondent for *The Blood-Horse*, said the trainer could be 'alternately reasonably convivial and completely taciturn.' Jockey Brooks...said 'I always liked Moody. Helluva horseman. He was hard to work for, sure. He'd sack you one day and hire you back the next.' "

Steve Brooks, Round Table's first regular rider, who had survived more than three decades of competition, died September 23, 1979, as the result of a training accident. Brooks was working as an exercise rider at Arlington Park when he was thrown from a horse, injuring his throat. Three weeks later while en route from Chicago to Florida, he was hospitalized in Louisville and underwent emergency surgery for a ruptured esophagus. Brooks died as a result of complications following the surgery. He was fifty-eight.

Bill Shoemaker, Round Table's "most regular" rider, retired from the saddle in 1989 with a world-record total of 8,833 wins. (Another paragon of extended excellence, Laffit Pincay Jr., who is still active, broke Shoemaker's record in December of 1999.) Shoemaker

enjoyed a successful training career that was cut short by the tragic auto accident of April 8, 1991, that left him a quadriplegic.

Travis Kerr passed away at age sixty-seven in Beverly Hills, California, in June of 1970, victim of a massive cerebral hemorrhage. This deprived the sport of a truly committed patron who had taken great joy in his horses' achievements both on and off the track. Kerr, who after Round Table's 1957 American Derby win at Arlington rushed to the barn and hotwalked his horse himself, once said, "One of the most wonderful things about racing is watching the little ones grow up. It gives you a feeling for the game you never find at the mutuel machines."

Kerr's proudest equine possession would survive him by seventeen years. Round Table was euthanized at age thirty-three on June 16, 1987, at Claiborne Farm.

After having been born within hours of each other five years earlier, Round Table and Bold Ruler had been reunited at Claiborne late in 1959. Bold Ruler arrived back home first, following his retirement in 1958. The one-time rivals proceeded to live in stalls across from each other in the stallion barn and for the dozen years until Bold Ruler's death in 1971 had adjoining paddocks on the beautiful Kentucky farm.

Bull Hancock's daughter Dell Hancock, who grew up at Claiborne and today serves as the farm's spokesperson, well remembers observing the old warrior.

"In his last years, Round Table lived in a paddock right behind my house here on the farm. Every evening, I'd grate up some carrots and go out to him. He'd see me coming and he'd take off on those little, old peg legs he had and hurry over. He was one of the kindest horses I've ever been around.

"I was too young to remember seeing Round Table race, but I got to be awfully fond of him during all the years we lived together," Hancock said.

Round Table was the sort of horse to ignite emotions like that, in people such as Dell Hancock and John Sosby, who started working at Claiborne two years after Round Table was foaled and, as the farm's general manager, sadly supervised the burial of his old pal in Claiborne's horse cemetery on a June day thirty-one years later.

There were thousands of others as well, including a bookmaking bar owner in Kenosha, Wisconsin, whose

epiphany one afternoon at Arlington Park evolved into a hearty admiration that for years saw Angelo Salerno loudly pronounce his preference whenever the subject of great horses arose.

When Angelo got excited, he talked in italics, and this is what he would say about Travis Kerr's tough little bay:

"There's *one* horse for me— *Round Table*! He worked hard *all* the time...He was like a little *machine*."

ROUND TABLE's
PEDIGREE

		Rose Prince, 1919	Prince **Palatine** Eglantine
	Prince Rose, 1928		
		Indolence, 1920	Gay Crusader Barrier
PRINCEQUILLO (GB), b, 1940			
		Papyrus, 1920	Tracery Miss Matty
	Cosquilla, 1933		
ROUND TABLE, bay colt, 1954		Quick Thought, 1918	White **Eagle** Mindful
		The Boss, 1910	Orby Southern Cross II
	Sir Cosmo, 1926		
		Ayn Hali, 1913	Desmond Lalla **Rookh**
KNIGHT'S DAUGHTER (GB), b, 1941			
		Friar Marcus, 1912	Cicero Prim **Nun**
	Feola, 1933		
		Aloe, 1926	Son-in-Law Alope

ROUND TABLE's RACE RECORD

Round Table

b. c. 1954, by Princequillo (Prince Rose)–Knight's Daughter, by Sir Cosmo

Lifetime record: 66 43 8 5 $1,749,869

Own.– Kerr Stable
Br – Claiborne Farm (Ky)
Tr.– W. Molter

31Oct59- 7Aqu	fst 2	:46^{3} 2:28^{4} 2:55 3:22^{1}	3↑	J C Gold Cup 110k	1	2	2^{4}	2$^{\frac12}$	3^{6}	2^{7}	Bailey PJ	124	b	1.70	--	Sword Dancr119^{7}RoundTable124$^{1\frac14}$Tudor Era124$^{2\frac14}$	No match	8
10Oct59- 7Aqu	fst 1⅝	:49^{1} 1:39^{2} 2:04^{1} 2:42^{3}	3↑	Manhattan H 58k	4	4	4$^{1\frac12}$	3$^{1\frac12}$	1^{hd}	1^{1}	Shoemaker W	132	b	*1.55	--	RoundTable132^{1}BaldEagle122$^{1\frac12}$Coloneast112^{2}	Brisk urging	11
26Sep59- 7Aqu	fst 1¼	:49^{1} 1:14^{1} 1:40 2:04^{2}	3↑	Woodward 109k	3	2	2$^{\frac12}$	2^{hd}	3$^{1\frac12}$	3$^{1\frac34}$	Shoemaker W	126	b	*.70	--	SwordDancer120^{hd}Hillsdale126$^{1\frac34}$RoundTable126^{5}	No excuse	4
19Sep59- 7Atl	fm 1 3/16Ⓣ	:47^{2} 1:11^{4} 1:36^{3} 1:55^{1}	3↑	U Nations H 100k	6	2	2^{3}	2$^{\frac12}$	1^{1}	1$^{1\frac14}$	Shoemaker W	136	b	*.80	97-03	RoundTable136$^{1\frac14}$Noureddin117$^{3\frac12}$Li'lFella120$^{1\frac12}$	Mild urging	10
7Sep59- 8AP	fst 1⅛	:47 1:10^{3} 1:35 1:47^{1}	3↑	Wash Park H 122k	2	5	5$^{6\frac34}$	4$^{3\frac12}$	1^{3}	1$^{6\frac12}$	Shoemaker W	132	b	*.70	106-04	RoundTable132$^{6\frac12}$Dunce114$^{\frac34}$BelluChf112^{hd}	Under mild urging	6
22Aug59- 8AP	fm 1 3/16Ⓣ	:46^{3} 1:10^{2} 1:35^{2} 1:53^{2}	3↑	Arlington H 125k	1	3	3^{4}	1^{1}	1$^{2\frac12}$	1^{hd}	Shoemaker W	132	b	*.80e	104-02	RndTable132^{hd}Manassas112^{nk}Noureddin109^{2}	Strong urging	9
15Aug59- 4AP	sf 1⅛Ⓣ	:48^{4} 1:13^{2} 1:39^{2} 1:51^{4}	3↑	Handicap 10000	5	2	2$^{1\frac12}$	2^{1}	2^{hd}	1^{nk}	Shoemaker W	132	b	*.80	83-17	RndTable132^{nk}TudorEra115$^{1\frac34}$TerraFirma110$^{1\frac12}$	Hand ridden	5
8Aug59- 8AP	sl 1	:23 :46 1:11^{2} 1:37	3↑	Equipoise Mile H 56k	1	7	6$^{6\frac14}$	6$^{8\frac12}$	3^{6}	3^{5}	Shoemaker W	132	b	*.90	80-23	BetterBee115^{1}BelleauChief114^{4}RoundTable132$^{2\frac14}$	Slow start	10
4Jly59- 8Was	fm 1⅛Ⓣ	:47 1:10^{3} 1:35 1:47^{1}	3↑	Stars & Stripes H 85k	4	2	2^{2}	2^{2}	1^{2}	1$^{3\frac14}$	Shoemaker W	132	b	*.70	107-00	RndTable132$^{3\frac14}$Noureddn110^{nk}TudorEr117$^{\frac12}$	Scored cleverly	9
25Jun59- 0Was	fm 1 1/16Ⓣ	:24^{2} :47^{3} 1:12 1:42^{3}	4↑	Exhibition 4k	3	1	1^{6}	1^{10}	1^{10}	1^{10}	Brooks S	0	b	-	97-07	Round Table0^{10}On the Job0^{1}Martini II0$^{3\frac14}$	Speed to spare	4
	Special exhibition purse run between 3rd and 4th races. No weights assigned. No wagering																	
13Jun59- 8Was	fst 1	:22^{2} :44^{4} 1:09^{1} 1:33^{2}	3↑	Citation H 56k	2	4	4^{4}	4$^{1\frac14}$	2^{hd}	1^{nk}	Brooks S	130	b	*.90	100-06	RoundTable130^{nk}Etonian104$^{3\frac14}$Charli'sSong112$^{2\frac14}$	Bore in,up	11
23Feb59- 7SA	sf 1½Ⓣ	:47^{4} 1:13^{2} 2:06^{2} 2:32^{2}	3↑	Wash Birthday H 60k	9	5	2$^{\frac12}$	9$^{7\frac14}$	15^{24}	16^{30}	Shoemaker W	134	b	*.50e	35-35	Hakuchikar109^{nk}Ansdo110$^{3\frac34}$Aorng107$^{1\frac14}$	Cut front left heel	16
24Jan59- 7SA	fm 1¼Ⓣ	:45^{3} 1:09^{4} 1:33^{4} 1:58^{2}	3↑	San Marcos H 28k	5	1	1$^{2\frac12}$	1^{2}	1^{5}	1^{5}	Shoemaker W	132	b	*.55e	102-00	RndTable132^{5}EddieSchmidt116^{1}AndrewAln115$^{\frac34}$	Won in hand	8
3Jan59- 7SA	fst 7f	:22^{4} :45 1:09^{2} 1:21^{4}	3↑	San Carlos H 56k	4	5	3^{1}	2^{hd}	2$^{\frac12}$	2^{hd}	Shoemaker W	132	b	*1.80	94-12	Hillsdale115^{hd}RoundTable132$^{2\frac14}$EddiSchmdt112$^{\frac34}$	Closed fast	10
11Oct58- 8Haw	fst 1¼	:46^{3} 1:10^{2} 1:35^{2} 1:59^{4}	3↑	Haw Gold Cup H 123k	6	2	2$^{1\frac14}$	1^{2}	1^{2}	1$^{2\frac14}$	Shoemaker W	126	wb	*.70	102-02	RndTable126$^{2\frac14}$Swoon'sSon123^{2}Ekb113^{nk}	Good lead in hand	6
27Sep58- 7Bel	sly 1¼	:46^{4} 1:10^{4} 1:35^{3} 2:01	3↑	Woodward 111k	1	1	2^{hd}	4$^{3\frac12}$	5$^{9\frac12}$	5^{17}	Arcaro E	126	wb	*.80	78-13	Clem126$^{\frac12}$Nadir120^{2}Reneged126^{9}	Had speed 6f,tired	7
13Sep58- 7Atl	fm 1 3/16Ⓣ	:47^{2} 1:11^{2} 1:36^{2} 1:54^{3}	3↑	U Nations H 100k	2	4	5^{4}	2^{2}	2^{1}	2$^{\frac12}$	Valenzuela I	130	wb	*.60	105-00	Clem113$^{\frac12}$Round Table130^{3}Combustion II115$^{\frac34}$	No excuse	12
8Sep58- 7Atl	fm 1 1/16Ⓣ	:23^{1} :46^{1} 1:11^{2} 1:43^{3}	3↑	Alw 5000	4	3	3^{3}	2$^{1\frac12}$	1^{hd}	1^{2}	Shoemaker W	128	wb	*.30	95-05	RoundTabl128^{2}St.Vncnt113^{nk}Rfty115^{hd}	Eased final strides	7
1Sep58- 8AP	fst 1	:22^{3} :45^{1} 1:09^{1} 1:34	3↑	Was Park H 139k	3	8	7$^{4\frac34}$	4$^{4\frac12}$	3^{4}	2$^{3\frac14}$	Shoemaker W	131	wb	*2.00e	99-02	Clem110$^{3\frac14}$Round Table131^{no}Nadir114^{6}	Rallying strongly	9
23Aug58- 8AP	fm 1 3/16Ⓣ	:47 1:11 1:36 1:54^{2}	3↑	Arlington H 85k	3	4	4^{3}	2^{hd}	1^{hd}	1$^{2\frac14}$	Shoemaker W	130	wb	*.90	99-09	RoundTable130$^{2\frac14}$Clem109$^{\frac34}$St.Vincent111$^{1\frac12}$	Drew away easily	8
9Aug58- 8AP	fst 1	:24 :46^{3} 1:10^{1} 1:34^{4}	3↑	Equipoise Mile H 133k	1	8	8^{7}	8$^{7\frac14}$	8$^{8\frac12}$	5^{4}	Shoemaker W	131	wb	*.90	94-11	Swoon'sSon129$^{\frac12}$Bardstown122$^{\frac12}$IndianCrk107$^{\frac12}$	In close early	10
19Jly58- 8AP	fm 1⅛Ⓣ	:48^{1} 1:12 1:36^{3} 1:48^{2}	3↑	Laurance Armour H 87k	1	3	4$^{2\frac12}$	4$^{1\frac12}$	2$^{1\frac12}$	1no	Hartack W	130	wb	*.70e	100-07	RndTable130^{no}Clem110$^{3\frac14}$HoopBnd118^{2}	Blocked off,just up	10
12Jly58- 8AP	fst 1⅛	:47 1:10^{4} 1:35^{4} 1:48^{3}	3↑	W Wright Mem H 85k	4	5	5$^{2\frac14}$	1^{hd}	1^{2}	2^{hd}	Longden J	130	wb	*.30	99-10	Bernburgoo109^{hd}RoundTable130$^{2\frac14}$ShnPc108^{5}	Good lead,tired	8
28Jun58- 8Was	fm 1 3/16Ⓣ	:46^{4} 1:10^{4} 1:36^{2} 1:54^{4}	3↑	Arch Ward H 56k	3	3	2$^{1\frac12}$	2^{1}	1$^{1\frac12}$	1$^{2\frac12}$	Shoemaker W	129	wb	*.30e	99-01	RoundTable129$^{2\frac12}$TallChiefII115$^{2\frac14}$Aysha106$^{2\frac14}$	Scored easily	9
20Jun58- 0Was	fm 1 1/16Ⓣ	:24^{3} :49 1:14^{1} 1:46^{4}	3↑	Alw 6000	3	3	3^{3}	2^{hd}	1$^{1\frac12}$	1^{2}	Valenzuela I	122	wb	-e	76-31	Round Table122^{2}Bernburgoo114^{3}Black Patch114$^{\frac34}$	Easily	5
	Special event run between 3rd and 4th races. No wagering																	
7Jun58- 7Hol	fst 1	:23^{1} :46^{1} 1:10^{1} 1:34^{3}	3↑	Argonaut H 53k	2	5	5$^{5\frac12}$	3^{3}	3^{2}	1no	Shoemaker W	132	wb	*.70	93-24	Round Table132^{no}How Now116$^{5\frac34}$Seaneen120^{3}	Up in time	6
24May58- 7Hol	fst 1 1/16	:23^{3} :47 1:10^{4} 1:41	3↑	Californian 108k	1	3	3$^{4\frac12}$	3^{2}	2^{3}	2$^{4\frac14}$	Shoemaker W	130	wb	*.15	86-14	Seaneen109$^{4\frac14}$RoundTable130^{3}Terrng115$^{4\frac12}$	Failed to respond	5
11May58-10AC	gd 1 1/16	:23 :46 1:11^{2} 1:41^{1}	3↑	Caliente H 51k	2	3	4$^{3\frac12}$	2^{hd}	1$^{3\frac12}$	1$^{9\frac14}$	Shoemaker W	126	w	*.10	105-15	RoundTable126$^{9\frac14}$WarMarshall105^{1}LikeMagic108$^{\frac34}$	Easy score	10
22Mar58- 7GP	fst 1¼	:47^{1} 1:11 1:35^{2} 1:59^{4}	3↑	Gulf Park H 110k	4	3	3$^{7\frac12}$	2^{2}	1$^{\frac12}$	1^{4}	Shoemaker W	130	wb	*.20	100-12	RoundTable130^{4}Meeting111^{nk}Oligrchy111^{2}	Speed in reserve	6
14Mar58- 7GP	fst 1 1/16	:23^{2} :46^{2} 1:10^{3} 1:41^{3}	4↑	Alw 10000	4	3	3^{5}	2$^{1\frac12}$	1$^{\frac12}$	1$^{3\frac12}$	Harmatz W	128	wb	*.25	102-11	RoundTable128$^{3\frac12}$Meeting111^{1}Bureaucracy109$^{2\frac12}$	Easily best	6
1Mar58- 7SA	fst 1¼	:45^{2} 1:09^{3} 1:34^{3} 1:59^{4}	3↑	S Anita H 135k	9	3	4^{2}	2^{hd}	1$^{\frac12}$	1$^{2\frac12}$	Shoemaker W	130	wb	*.15	101-09	RoundTable130$^{2\frac12}$Terrang119$^{3\frac12}$Porterhous120^{2}	Under a drive	9
15Feb58- 7SA	fst 1⅛	:46^{2} 1:10^{1} 1:34^{3} 1:46^{4}	3↑	San Antonio H 56k	3	6	4$^{2\frac12}$	1^{hd}	1^{2}	1$^{3\frac12}$	Shoemaker W	130	wb	*.45	103-11	Round Table130$^{3\frac12}$Mystic Eye108$^{1\frac12}$Promised Land116$^{\frac12}$	Easily	9

Copyrighted © 2000 by Daily Racing Form, Inc. Reprinted from the book "Champions" (DRF Press)

ROUND TABLE's RACE RECORD CONTINUED

25Jan58- 7SA	fst	1¼	:472	1:113	1:362	2:014	S Anita Maturity 156k	5	1	13	11½	13	14½	Harmatz W	126wb	*.20	91-18	Rnd Table1264½Seaneen117¾Promised Land1252¾	Easing up	6
11Jan58- 7SA	fst	1 1/16	:24	:471	1:111	1:421	San Fernando 27k	3	1	13	14	16	14¼	Shoemaker W	130wb	*.25	93-13	RndTable1304¼TheSearcher114½Seaneen124hd	Eased at end	6
28Dec57- 7SA	fst	7f	:231	:454	1:094	1:22	Malibu Sequet 28k	4	6	53	31½	1½	1hd	Shoemaker W	130wb	*.15e	93-11	RoundTable130hdSeaneen1143¼MystcEy122nk	Brisk hand ride	8
9Nov57- 7GS	gd	1¼	:471	1:111	1:364	2:013	3↑ Trenton H 82k	2	2	28	33½	35	310¾	Harmatz W	124wb	1.70	86-14	BoldRuler1222¼GallantMan1248½RoundTable124	Tired badly	3
1Nov57- 0GS	sly	1 70	:23	:472	1:123	1:413	Alw 6000	1	2	21½	1½	15	18	Shoemaker W	126wb	-	89-16	RoundTble1268CommdreCurt11111HoosierHony108	Breezing	3
	Special race run between the 4th and 5th races. No wagering																			
12Oct57- 8Haw	fst	1¼	:461	1:103	1:351	2:001	3↑ Haw Gold Cup H 126k	1	2	21½	2hd	1hd	13	Harmatz W	121wb	*.70	102-08	RndTbl1213Swoon'sSon1282½Fnd1192½	Drew clear with ease	6
4Oct57- 0Haw	fst	1 1/16	:232	:472	1:114	1:434	Alw 5000	2	1	11½	13	14	17	Shoemaker W	126wb	-	93-18	Round Table1267Hundred Grand1116Mr. Donmar1111½	Easily	4
	Special race run between the 8th and 9th races. No wagering																			
14Sep57- 7Atl	fm	1 3/16Ⓣ	:473	1:12	1:372	1:561	3↑ U Nations H 100k	11	4	1hd	2hd	1hd	1no	Shoemaker W	118wb	*.70	98-02	RoundTable118noTudorEra1122Find1222	Stumbled st.,gamely	11
31Aug57- 8Was	fm	1 3/16Ⓣ	:473	1:114	1:37	1:55	American Derby 145k	8	1	11½	13	13	14	Shoemaker W	126wb	*1.00	98-12	Round Table1264Iron Liege1263½Ekaba1202	Very easy score	8
20Aug57- 0Was	fm	1 1/16Ⓣ	:25	:49	1:13	1:433	Alw 5000	4	1	2½	21½	21	11¼	Shoemaker W	124wb	-e	92-08	RoundTable1241¼Ekaba113.52¼MartiniII11215	An easy score	4
	Exhibition race run before 1st race. No wagering																			
20Jly57- 7Hol	fst	1¼	:454	1:094	1:344	2:003	Westerner 115k	8	5	31	13	15	12	Shoemaker W	129wb	*.15	90-12	RoundTable1292Irisher110noJoePrice1187	Eased at the end	8
13Jly57- 7Hol	fst	1¼	:452	1:091	1:334	1:583	3↑ Hol Gold Cup H 162k	8	4	2hd	11½	14	13¼	Shoemaker W	109wb	*1.40	100-15	Round Table1093¼Porterhouse1192Find1187	Drew out	11
6Jly57- 7Hol	fst	1⅛	:461	1:102	1:351	1:474	Cinema H 47k	1	2	1½	1hd	14	14	Shoemaker W	130wb	*.20	95-14	RoundTable1304JoePrice1142¾Seanen1092¾	Speed in reserve	7
15Jun57- 7Hol	fst	1 1/16	:231	:46	1:10	1:41	El Dorado H 37k	5	3	21	1½	14	17	Taniguchi G	126wb	*.25	90-16	Round Table1267Joe Price1154Playtown107hd	Easy score	6
30May57- 7Hol	fst	1	:222	:452	1:093	1:342	©Will Rogers 28k	9	1	42½	2hd	13	13½	Neves R	122wb	*.45	94-11	RoundTable1223½JoePrice1182¾Mqult1111¼	Driving,bore out	9
25May57- 7Hol	fst	1 1/16	:222	:451	1:093	1:402	3↑ Californian 116k	4	4	43½	2hd	2½	21½	Neves R	105wb	2.85	91-20	SocialClmbr1191½RoundTbl1054½Fnd119nk	Led between calls	12
4May57- 7CD	fst	1¼	:47	1:112	1:364	2:021	Ky Derby 152k	3	4	43½	42	41	32¾	Neves R	126wb	3.60	93-12	IronLiege126noGallantMan1262¾RoundTable1263	Held well	9
25Apr57- 6Kee	fst	1⅛	:48	1:11	1:343	1:472	Blue Grass 31k	1	1	11½	11½	12½	16	Neves R	126wb	*1.00	108-02	Round Table1266One-Eyed King1212Manteau1211¼	Much best	6
6Apr57- 8BM	fst	1 1/16	:224	:462	1:102	1:413	BM Derby 52k	3	2	12	11	13	14½	Neves R	122wb	1.80	96-13	Round Table1224½Swirling Abbey1226Irisher1221¼	Easily	6
11Mar57- 7SA	hy	1 1/16	:241	:484	1:144	1:491	San Bernardino H 28k	9	2	21½	21½	22	58½	Longden J	122wb	*.65e	49-34	LightningJack112¾MysticEye1113¼RoyalHeir1151	Faltered	9
2Mar57- 7SA	sl	1⅛	:474	1:132	1:414	1:541	S Anita Derby 98k	11	3	33½	22	1hd	3hd	Longden J	118wb	*1.30e	70-30	SirWilliam118hdSwirlingAbbey118noRoundTabl1182½	Ran out	13
	Previously trained by M. Jolley																			
16Feb57- 8Hia	fst	7f	:224	:451	1:092	1:222	Alw 5000	6	1	14	16	16	16	Brooks S	126wb	7.05	98-10	Round Table1266Lucky Dip1142½Jet Colonel1235	Much best	9
	Previously owned by Claiborne Farm																			
9Feb57- 5Hia	fst	1 1/16	:232	:47	1:112	1:424	Alw 10000	6	5	64	65¾	68½	611	Brooks S	113wb	6.45	90-15	IronLiege1142¼Gen.Duke112hdMssl1244	Could not keep pace	7
19Jan57- 7Hia	fst	6f	:221	:451		1:10	©Hibiscus 26k	7	3	3½	118	118	1010	Brooks S	122 w	10.60	85-09	Gallant Man117½Missile1221½King Hairan1221½	Speed,tired	13
3Nov56- 6CD	fst	7f	:232	:464	1:113	1:25	Alw 7500	9	4	127¾	139¾	136¼	87¼	Brooks S	122 w	*1.00	81-14	Charlie'sSong113nkSrPutnm107nkEkb113hd	Wide most of way	14
20Oct56- 6Kee	fst	*7f				1:264	Breeders' Futurity 66k	4	7	75¼	76½	32	1½	Brooks S	122 w	2.50	99-04	RoundTable122½Missile1221Tranquil122¾	Under brisk drive	10
11Oct56- 5Kee	fst	6f	:224	:454		1:101	©Alw 5000	2	1	23	21½	21½	11½	Brooks S	119 w	*.40	99-08	RoundTable1191½DixieDudley1163CardinalSin1161½	Handily	5
6Aug56- 7Was	fst	6f	:222	:452		1:102	George Woolf Mem 18k	6	-	-	-	-	-	Brooks S	120 w	2.10	- -	Smart Phil114hdJet Colonel1175Federal Hill1144		9
	Stumbled leaving gate,lost rider																			
21Jly56- 8AP	sly	6f	:223	:46		1:121	Arl Futurity 140k	3	3	32	44½	410	46½	Brooks S	122 w	6.50	76-30	GreekGame1225JetColonel122¾Etonian117¾	Fell back early	7
4Jly56- 7AP	gd	5½f	:221	:454	:59	1:053	Hyde Park 22k	3	5	45¼	47½	310	25	Brooks S	122 w	2.10	85-19	GreekGame1225RoundTable122nkJetColonel118½	Closed fast	8
28Jun56- 3AP	fst	5f	:222	:454		:583	Alw 3500	1	1	4nk	2hd	11½	12	Brooks S	118 w	*.90	97-11	Round Table1182Jet Colonel1181½Kid Jr.1202	Ridden out	6
25Apr56- 6Kee	fst	*4f				:493	Lafayette 20k	1	1		11	1hd	1½	Brooks S	117 w	3.80	99-02	Round Table117½Jet Colonel117hdChookoss1172	Hard urged	9
14Apr56- 3Kee	sly	*4f				:503	Md Sp Wt	1	1		11	11	12½	Brooks S	118 w	*1.20	94-05	Round Table1182½Pandean1188Yonshu113no	Under mild drive	8
24Feb56- 3Hia	fst	3f	:214			:332	Alw 5000	7	5			43	42	Brooks S	116 w	14.50	- -	Myla111½OlympiaJet119½LuckyMistake1161	Bumped at start	14

Copyrighted © 2000 by Daily Racing Form, Inc. Reprinted from the book "Champions" (DRF Press)

Index

Photo Credits

Cover photo: (The Blood-Horse)

Page 1: Round Table head shot (The Blood-Horse); Round Table comeback shot (The Blood-Horse)

Page 2: Princequillo (The Blood-Horse); Knight's Daughter (J.C. Skeets Meadors)

Page 3: Round Table in winner's circle; A.B. Hancock Jr.; Round Table with the Kerrs, Bill Molter, and Juan Alaniz (all The Blood-Horse)

Page 4: Bill Molter with Round Table (Bert and Richard Morgan); Moody Jolley (The Blood-Horse)

Page 5: Bill Shoemaker with Round Table (The Blood-Horse); Steve Brooks aboard Round Table (J.C. Skeets Meadors); Ralph Neves (Santa Anita)

Page 6: Round Table winning the Lafayette Stakes and Breeders' Futurity (both J.C. Skeets Meadors)

Page 7: Round Table in Blue Grass post parade, winning the Blue Grass (both Keeneland Association); the Kentucky Derby final turn (Courier-Journal and Louisville Times)

Page 8: Round Table winning the American Derby, the Will Rogers Stakes, and the Westerner (all The Blood-Horse)

Page 9: Winning the Malibu, the San Fernando, and the Arch Ward (all The Blood-Horse); Winning the Argonaut (Hollywood Park)

Page 10: Winning the Laurance Armour (The Blood-Horse); Winning the Hawthorne Gold Cup (Hawthorne Race Course); Round Table with Juan Alaniz (Bert and Richard Morgan)

Page 11: Winning the San Marcos and Arlington handicaps (The Blood-Horse); Winning the Citation Handicap (Balmoral)

Page 12: Round Table working out (Allen F. Brewer Jr.); Winning the United Nations (Turfotos); Winning the Manhattan (Bert and Richard Morgan)

Page 13: Round Table conformation (Allen F. Brewer Jr.); Arriving at Claiborne (J.C. Skeets Meadors)

Page 14: Drumtop, Royal Glint (both by Jim Raftery/Turfotos); King Pellinore (Santa Anita)

Page 15: He's a Smoothie (Jim Raftery/Turfotos); King's Bishop (Paul Schafer/NYRA); Apalachee (Alec Russell)

Page 16: Round Table at Claiborne (J.C. Skeets Meadors); Gravestone (Barbara D. Livingston)

J ohn McEvoy, a graduate of the University of Wisconsin, is a former newspaper reporter and college English teacher who subsequently served as Midwest editor, then senior writer for *Daily Racing Form*.

He is the author of *Great Horse Racing Mysteries* and co-author with his daughter, Julia McEvoy, of *Women in Racing: In Their Own Words*. McEvoy also is the author of the 1995 book *Through the Pages of Daily Racing Form*, an historical overview of American Thoroughbred racing based on material that had appeared in that newspaper's first one hundred years.

He has published a book of poetry and his *Stiffereeno*, a crime novel with a horse racing theme, was to be published in 2002. He and his wife, Judy, live in Evanston, Illinois; they have three children and three grandchildren.

Forthcoming titles
in the

THOROUGHBRED
Legends®

series:

War Admiral

Exterminator

Carry Back

Available titles:

Man o' War

Dr. Fager

Citation

Go for Wand

Seattle Slew

Forego

Native Dancer

Nashua

Spectacular Bid

John Henry

Personal Ensign

Sunday Silence

Ruffian

Swaps

Affirmed and Alydar

www.thoroughbredlegends.com